Timeless Quotations on

SUCCESS

D1385973

POCKET POSITIVES™

Timeless Quotations on

SUCCESS

Compiled by John Cook

Fairview Press
Minneapolis

Published by Fairview Press, 2450 Riverside Avenue South, Minneapolis, MN 55454.

Library of Congress Cataloging-in-Publication Data
Timeless quotations on success / compiled by John Cook.
      p.   cm. -- (Pocket positives)
    ISBN 1-57749-062-2 (pbk.: alk. paper)
    1. Success--Quotations, maxims, etc. I. Cook,
John, 1939–   . II. Series.
PN6084.S78T56   1997
646.7--dc21   97-31299
                                        CIP

First Printing: November 1997
Printed in the United States of America
01 00 99 98 97   7 6 5 4 3 2 1

Cover design: Laurie Duren

Publisher's Note: The publications of Fairview Press, including the Pocket Positives™ series, do not necessarily reflect the philosophy of Fairview Health System or its treatment programs.

For a free catalogue, call toll-free 1–800–544–8207, or visit our website at http://www.Press.Fairview.org.

for Freddi, Blake, Brian, and Timmy

CONTENTS

INTRODUCTION

THE BOOKS IN THE POCKET POSITIVES™ SERIES originated as a selection of life-affirming quotations I compiled for my nephews and niece for Christmas 1989.

Because I was concerned that one of them was too young for it, I wrote in a letter that accompanied the collection, "just put it away in a safe place until you're ready for it." To address the question of how someone would know they were "ready," I wrote:

"You'll be ready the first time things don't go the way you want them to, the first time you doubt your ability to do something, the first time you're tempted to quit or give up, the first time you actually fail at something.

"You'll be ready the first time you doubt a friend, or think you can't trust anyone.

"You'll be ready the first time you have to make an important decision, or choice.

"You'll be ready the first time you're afraid of something, or worried.

"You'll know when you're ready. When you are, these thoughts should give you the courage and confidence and spirit you need ... and they'll remind you of the wonder and the joy of life, regardless of how dark things seem at the moment.

"I know they will.... They always have for me."

So, in addition to being a resource for researchers, writers, students, and professionals, I hope this book—and all the books in the Pocket Positives™ series—will provide comfort and inspiration for the casual browser or reader.

• • •

Numerous questions and concerns about accuracy confront anyone who compiles quotations. Take, for example, differences in the spelling of sources' names. The same famous Russian novelist has had his name spelled "Dostoevski," "Dostoievski," and "Dostoyevsky."

The formality required to identify sources is another issue. The Spanish Jesuit writer Baltasar Gracian Y Morales, for example, is more commonly referred to as "Baltasar Gracian," or simply "Gracian." And some sources are almost universally referred to by only one name, usually in the interest of brevity, and because it would be difficult to confuse them with anyone else. "Crebillion," for example, is used for Prosper Jolyot de Crebillion, the French dramatic poet.

And, of course, through the years many exact quotations—and even more that are very similar—have been attributed to more than one source.

I have made every effort to present each quotation as accurately as possible, and to recognize and honor the appropriate source. In particularly demanding situations, the language and sources cited are those most often used by other compilers and editors. Where it was impossible to verify the accuracy or source of a quotation, I have included it anyway if I believed that the usefulness of the quotation outweighed the demands of scholarly rigor.

Part One

Success

BASIC SUCCESS TECHNIQUES

The successful person is the individual who forms the habit of doing what the failing person doesn't like to do.
—Donald Riggs

The secret of every man who has ever been successful lies in the fact that he formed the bait of doing those things that failures don't like to do.
—A. Jackson King

Nature gave men two ends—one to sit on, and one to think with. Ever since then man's success or failure has been dependent on the one he used most.
—George R. Kirkpatrick

I've been polite and I've always shown up. Somebody asked me if I had any advice for young people entering the business. I said: "Yeah, show up."
—Tom T. Hall

Make yourself indispensable and you'll be moved up. Act as if you're indispensable and you'll be moved out.

—Unknown

What is the recipe for successful achievement? To my mind there are just four essential ingredients: Choose a career you love.... Give it the best there is in you.... Seize your opportunities.... And be a member of the team.

—Benjamin F. Fairless

Vacillating people seldom succeed. They seldom win the solid respect of their fellows. Successful men and women are very careful in reaching decisions, and very persistent and determined in action thereafter.

—L.G. Elliott

The wise man puts all his eggs in one basket and watches the basket.

—Andrew Carnegie

Many people have the ambition to succeed; they may even have a special aptitude for their job. And yet they do not move ahead. Why? Perhaps they think that since they can master the job, there is no need to master themselves.

—John Stevenson

I know the price of success: dedication, hard work and an unremitting devotion to the things you want to see happen.

—Frank Lloyd Wright

A double-minded man is unstable in all his ways.… A determinate purpose in life and a steady adhesion to it through all disadvantages are indispensable conditions of success.

—William M. Punshion

The secret of success in life is for a man to be ready for his opportunity when it comes.

—Benjamin Disraeli

We may fail of our happiness, strive we ever so bravely, but we are less likely to fail if we measure with judgement our chances and our capabilities.

—Agnes Repplier

There are no secrets to success. It is the result of preparation, hard work, learning from failure.

—General Colin L. Powell

To be ambitious for wealth, and yet always expecting to be poor; to be always doubting your ability to get what you long for, is like trying to reach east by traveling west. There is no philosophy which will help man to succeed when he is always doubting his ability to do so, and thus attracting failure. No matter how hard you work for success, if your thought is saturated with the fear of failure, it will kill your efforts, neutralize your endeavors and make success impossible.

—Charles Baudouin

Before everything else, getting ready is
the secret of success.

> —Henry Ford

Success is that old ABC—Ability, Breaks
and Courage.

> —Charles Luckman

If one advances confidently in the
direction of his dreams, and endeavors to
live the life which he has imaged, he will
meet with success unexpected in
common hours.

> —Henry David Thoreau

The conditions of conquest are always
easy. We have but to toil awhile, endure
awhile, believe always, and never turn
back.

> —Marcus Annaeus Seneca

The very first step towards success in any
occupation is to become interested in it.

> —Sir William Osler

Without ambition one starts nothing. Without work one finishes nothing. The prize will not be sent to you. As to methods there may be a million and then some, but the principles are few. The man who grasps principles can successfully select his own methods. The man who tries methods, ignoring principles, is sure to have trouble.

—Ralph Waldo Emerson

I studied the lives of great men and famous women; and I found that the men and women who got to the top were those who did the jobs they had in hand, with everything they had of energy and enthusiasm and hard work.

—Harry S. Truman

Three outstanding qualities make for success: judgement, industry, health. And the greatest of these is judgement.

—William Maxwell Aitken,
Lord Beaverbrook

Success is blocked by concentrating on it and planning for it.… Success is shy—it won't come out while you're watching.
—Tennessee Williams

I cannot give you the formula for success, but I can give you the formula for failure, which is—try to please everybody.
—Herbert Bayard Swope

Success follows doing what you want to do. There is no other way to be successful.
—Malcolm Forbes

Always aim for achievement, and forget about success.
—Helen Hayes

Thirteen virtues necessary for true success: temperance, silence, order, resolution, frugality, industry, sincerity, justice, moderation, cleanliness, tranquility, chastity, and humility.
—Benjamin Franklin

Put your heart, mind, intellect and soul even to your smallest acts. This is the secret of success.

—Swami Sivananda

Four steps to achievement: plan purposefully, prepare prayerfully, proceed positively, pursue persistently.

—William A. Ward

Success, which is something so simple in the end, is made up of thousands of things, we never fully know what.

—Rainer Maria Rilke

The man who will use his skill and constructive imagination to see how much he can give for a dollar, instead of how little he can give for a dollar, is bound to succeed.

—Henry Ford

Self-trust is the first secret of success.

—Ralph Waldo Emerson

THE IMPORTANCE OF INTERPERSONAL RELATIONS

Whatever your grade or position, if you know how and when to speak, and when to remain silent, your chances of real success are proportionately increased.

—Ralph C. Smedley

No matter how much a man can do, no matter how engaging his personality may be, he will not advance far in business if he cannot work through others.

—John Craig

The art of dealing with people is the foremost secret of successful men. A man's success in handling people is the very yardstick by which the outcome of his whole life's work is measured.

—Paul C. Packe

The way to rise is to obey and please.

—Ben Johnson

The most important single ingredient in the formula of success is knowing how to get along with people.

—Theodore Roosevelt

The ability to form friendships, to make people believe in you and trust you is one of the few absolutely fundamental qualities of success. Selling, buying, negotiating are so much smoother and easier when the parties enjoy each other's confidence. The young man who can make friends quickly will find that he will glide, instead of stumble, through life.

—John J. McGuirk

Skill is fine, and genius is splendid, but the right contacts are more valuable than either.

—Sir Archibald McIndoe

THE IMPORTANCE OF DESIRE, ENTHUSIASM, ZEAL, OPTIMISM, AND ENERGY

A man can succeed at almost anything
for which he has unlimited enthusiasm.
—Charles M. Schwab

The world belongs to the energetic.
—Ralph Waldo Emerson

Sometimes success is due less to ability
than to zeal.
—Charles Buxton

There is a passion for perfection which
you rarely see fully developed; but you
may note this fact, that in successful lives
it is never wholly lacking.
—Bliss Carman

Flaming enthusiasm, backed up by horse
sense and persistence, is the quality that
most frequently makes for success.
—Dale Carnegie

We would accomplish many more things
if we did not think of them as impossible.
—C. Malesherbez

Someone's always saying, "It's not
whether you win or lose," but if you feel
that way, you're as good as dead.
—James Caan

Many of the most successful men I have
known have never grown up. They have
retained bubbling-over boyishness. They
have relished wit, they have indulged in
humor. They have not allowed "dignity"
to depress them into moroseness.
Youthfulness of spirit is the twin brother
of optimism, and optimism is the stuff of
which American business success is
fashioned. Resist growing up!
—B.C. Forbes

Success is going from failure to failure
without loss of enthusiasm.
—Sir Winston Churchill

If you have the will to win, you have achieved half your success; if you don't, you have achieved half your failure.

—David V. A. Ambrose

To bring one's self to a frame of mind and to the proper energy to accomplish things that require plain hard work continuously is the one big battle that everyone has. When this battle is won for all time, then everything is easy.

—Thomas A. Buckner

Always bear in mind that your own resolution to success is more important than any other one thing.

—Abraham Lincoln

The real secret of success is enthusiasm. Yes, more than enthusiasm, I would say excitement. I like to see men get excited. When they get excited, they make a success of their lives.

—Walter Chrysler

Faith that the thing can be done is essential to any great achievement.
—Thomas N. Carruther

Morale is the greatest single factor in successful wars.
—Dwight D. Eisenhower

The will to conquer is the first condition of victory.
—Marshal Ferdinand Foch

It is fatal to enter any war without the will to win it.
—General Douglas MacArthur

Enthusiasm for one's goal lessens the disagreeableness of working toward it.
—Thomas Eakins

To burn always with this hard gem-like flame, to maintain this ecstasy, is success in life.
—Walter Pater

The measure of an enthusiasm must be taken between interesting events. It is between bites that the lukewarm angler loses heart.

—Edwin Way Teale

Every man is enthusiastic at times. One man has enthusiasm for thirty minutes, another man has it for thirty days. But it is the man who has it for thirty years who makes a success in life.

—Edward B. Butler

A wise man will make more opportunities than he finds.

—Francis Bacon

We can accomplish almost anything within our ability if we but think that we can!

—George Matthew Adams

Man never rises to great truths without enthusiasm.

—Vauvenargues

Optimism is essential to achievement
and it is also the foundation of courage
and of true progress.
>—Nicholas Murray Butler

I rate enthusiasm even above professional
skill.
>—Sir Edward Appleton

He did it with all his heart, and prospered.
>—The Bible, II Chronicles

What a man accomplishes in a day
depends upon the way in which he
approaches his tasks. When we accept
tough jobs as a challenge to our ability
and wade into them with joy and
enthusiasm, miracles can happen. When
we do our work with a dynamic conquering spirit, we get things done.
>—Arland Gilbert

Success is due less to ability than to zeal.
>—Charles Buxton

Nothing great was ever achieved without enthusiasm.

> —Ralph Waldo Emerson

Do it big or stay in bed.

> —Larry Kelly

If you're not happy every morning when you get up, leave for work, or start to work at home, if you're not enthusiastic about doing that, you're not going to be successful.

> —Donald M. Kendall

A strong passion for any object will ensure success, for the desire of the end will point out the means.

> —William Hazlitt

The method of the enterprising is to plan with audacity and execute with vigor.

> —Christian Bovee

SELF-RELIANCE AND SUCCESS

If you want to succeed, you must make
your own opportunities as you go.
—John B. Gough

Every man is the architect of his own
fortune.
—Sallust

Man is still responsible.... His success
lies not with the stars, but with himself.
He must carry on the fight of self-correc-
tion and discipline.
—Frank Curtis Williams

If, after all, men cannot always make his-
tory have a meaning, they can always act
so that their own lives have one.
—Albert Camus

The brave man carves out his fortune, and
every man is the sum of his own works.
—Miguel de Cervantes

No one can help you in holding a good job except Old Man You.

—Edgar Watson Howe

Under normal periods, any man's success hinges about five percent on what others do for him and 95 percent on what he does.

—James A. Worsham

The people who get on in this world are the people who get up and look for the circumstances they want, and, if they can't find them, make them.

—George Bernard Shaw

If a man wants his dreams to come true, he must wake up.

—Unknown

No man will succeed unless he is ready to face and overcome difficulties and prepared to assume responsibilities.

—William J.H. Boetcker

Men at some time are masters of their
fates.
—William Shakespeare

Pa, he always said a man had to look spry
for himself, because nobody would do it
for him; your opportunities didn't come
knocking around, you had to hunt them
down and hog-tie them.
—Louis L'Amour

Destiny is not a matter of chance, it is a
matter of choice; it is not a thing to be
waited for, it is a thing to be achieved.
—William J. Bryan

We Must Take Risks to Succeed

The men who have done big things are those who were not afraid to attempt big things, who were not afraid to risk failure in order to gain success.

—B.C. Forbes

If the risk-reward ratio is right, you can make big money buying trouble.

—Unknown

He that would have fruit must climb the tree.

—Thomas Fuller

All great reforms require one to dare a lot to win a little.

—William L. O'Neill

If you limit your actions in life to things that nobody can possibly find fault with, you will not do much.

—Charles Lutwidge Dodgson

Great deeds are usually wrought at great risks.

—Herodotus

The ambitious climbs high and perilous stairs and never cares how to come down; the desire of rising hath swallowed up his fear of a fall.

—Thomas Adams

To get profit without risk, experience without danger and reward without work is as impossible as it is to live without being born.

—A.P. Gouthey

Every noble acquisition is attended with its risks; he who fears to encounter the one must not expect to obtain the other.

—Metastasio

The method of the enterprising is to plan with audacity and execute with vigor.

—Christian Bovee

What isn't tried won't work.

—Claude McDonald

Only those who dare to fail greatly can ever achieve greatly.

—Robert F. Kennedy

He that is overcautious will accomplish little.

—J.C.F. von Schiller

No one reaches a high position without daring.

—Publilius Syrus

I don't think about risks much. I just do what I want to do. If you gotta go, you gotta go.

—Miss Lillian Carter

Don't be afraid to take a big step if one is indicated. You can't cross a chasm in two small jumps.

—David Lloyd George

Progress always involves risks. You can't steal second base and keep your foot on first.
—Frederick B. Wilcox

It is impossible to win the great prizes of life without running risks.
—Theodore Roosevelt

You can't expect to hit the jackpot if you don't put a few nickels in the machine.
—Flip Wilson

Who dares nothing, need hope for nothing.
—J.C.F. von Schiller

Behold the turtle. He makes progress only when he sticks his neck out.
—James Bryant Conant

Nothing ventured, nothing gained.
—Unknown

You can't catch trout with dry breeches.
—Spanish proverb

WE CAN'T SUCCEED WITHOUT COURAGE

Because a fellow has failed once or twice or a dozen times, you don't want to set him down as a failure till he's dead or loses his courage—and that's the same thing.

—George Horace Lorimer

Whatever you do, you need courage.... To map out a course of action and follow it to an end requires some of the same courage which a soldier needs.

—Ralph Waldo Emerson

Courage permits the caliber of performance to continue at its peak, until the finish line is crossed.

—Stuart Walker

To see what is right, and not do it, is want of courage.

—Confucius

What is more mortifying than to feel
that you have missed the plum for want
of courage to shake the tree?
                    —Logan Pearsall Smith

It takes vision and courage to create—it
takes faith and courage to prove.
                    —Owen D. Young

No great thing comes to any man unless
he has courage.
                    —Cardinal James Gibbons

Courage and perseverance have a magical
talisman, before which difficulties
disappear, and obstacles vanish into air.
                    —John Quincy Adams

Have the courage of your desire.
                    —George R. Gissing

Great things are done more through
courage than through wisdom.
                    —German proverb

Failure is only postponed success as long as courage "coaches" ambition. The habit of persistence is the habit of victory.

—Herbert Kaufman

To persevere, trusting in what hopes he has, is courage. The coward despairs.

—Euripides

There are a lot of fellas with all the ability it takes to play in the major leagues, but they never make it, they always get stuck in the minor leagues because they haven't got the guts to make the climb.

—Cookie Lavagetto

You will never do anything in this world without courage.

—James Lane Allen

It takes as much courage to have tried and failed as it does to have tried and succeeded.

—Anne Morrow Lindbergh

Where there is a brave man, in the thickest of the fight, there is the post of honor.
—Henry David Thoreau

Whenever you see a successful business, someone once made a courageous decision.
—Peter Drucker

Courage to start and willingness to keep everlasting at it are the requisites for success.
—Alonzo Newton Benn

One of the biggest factors in success is the courage to undertake something.
—James A. Worsham

It is weak and despicable to go on wanting things and not trying to get them.
—Joanna Field

WORK AND SUCCESS

Nothing worthwhile comes easily. Half effort does not produce half results. It produces no results. Work, continuous work and hard work, is the only way to accomplish results that last.

—Hamilton Holt

If a man wakes up famous he hasn't been sleeping.

—Wes Izzard

Success is dependent on effort.

—Sophocles

Success comes before work only in the dictionary.

—Unknown

Striving for success without hard work is like trying to harvest where you haven't planted.

—David Bly

Sweat plus sacrifice equals success.
                    —Charles O. Finley

Success usually comes to those who are
too busy to be looking for it.
                    —Henry David Thoreau

In all human affairs there are *efforts*, and
there are *results*, and the strength of the
effort is the measure of the result.
                    —James Lane Allen

We Must Work on
the Right Things

It is no use saying "we are doing our
best." You have got to succeed in doing
what is necessary.
> —Sir Winston Churchill

Many people who wonder why they
don't amount to more than they do have
good stuff in them, and are energetic,
persevering, and have ample opportunities.
It is all a case of trimming the useless
branches and throwing the whole force
of power into the development of something that counts.
> Walter J. Johnston

Will you be satisfied with the fruit of
your life's work? Will the efforts you are
making now bring you satisfaction when
the things of time are receding, and
eternity looms ahead?
> —Raymond L. Cox

SUCCESS AND CHARACTER

Character is the real foundation of all worthwhile success.

> —John Hays Hammond

Some men succeed by what they know; some by what they do; and a few by what they are.

> —Elbert Hubbard

Try not to become a man of success, but rather a man of value.

> —Albert Einstein

If a man be self-controlled, truthful, wise, and resolute, is there aught that can stay out of reach of such a man?

> —*The Panchatantra*

Success seems to be that which forms the distinction between confidence and conceit.

> —Charles Caleb Colton

The common idea that success spoils
people by making them vain, egotistic,
and self-complacent is erroneous; on the
contrary, it makes them, for the most
part, humble, tolerant, and kind. Failure
makes people cruel and bitter.
—W. Somerset Maugham

It is abundantly clear that success tends
to negate humility.
—Landrum P. Leavell

Character cannot be developed in ease
and quiet. Only through experience of
trial and suffering can the soul be
strengthened, vision cleared, ambition
inspired, and success achieved.
—Helen Keller

To Succeed, We Must Learn to Admit and Accept Failure

One of the first businesses of a sensible man is to know when he is beaten, and to leave off fighting at once.

—Samuel Butler

If you can't accept losing, you can't win.

—Vince Lombardi

You can't have any successes unless you can accept failure.

—George Cukor

We have fought this fight as long, and as well, as we know how. We have been defeated … there is now but one course to pursue. We must accept the situation.

—Robert E. Lee

An error gracefully acknowledged is a victory won.

—Caroline L. Gascoigne

The most considerable difference I note among men is not in their readiness to fall into error, but in their readiness to acknowledge these inevitable lapses.
—Thomas Henry Huxley

The man who can own up to his error is greater than he who merely knows how to avoid making it.
—Cardinal De Retz

I have made mistakes, but I have never made the mistake of claiming that I never made one.
—James Gordon Bennett

WE MUST PERSEVERE TO BE SUCCESSFUL

I am not the smartest or most talented person in the world, but I succeeded because I keep going, and going, and going.

—Sylvester Stallone

I know the price of success: dedication, hard work and an unremitting devotion to the things you want to see happen.

—Frank Lloyd Wright

Victory belongs to the most persevering.

—Napoleon Bonaparte

Success generally depends upon knowing how long it takes to succeed.

—Charles de Montesquieu

Success seems to be largely a matter of hanging on after others have let go.

—William Feather

Call the roll in your memory of conspicuously successful business giants and … you will be struck by the fact that almost every one of them encountered inordinate difficulties sufficient to crush all but the gamest of spirits. Edison went hungry many times before he became famous.

—B.C. Forbes

The heights by great men reached and
   kept
Were not attained by sudden flight,
But they, while their companions slept
Were toiling upward in the night.

—Henry Wadsworth Longfellow

If you wish success in life, make perseverance your bosom friend.

—Joseph Addison

If at first you don't succeed, try, try, try again.

—W.E. Hickson

They who are the most persistent, and work in the true spirit, will invariably be the most successful.

—Samuel Smiles

If at first you don't succeed, you're running about average.

—M.H. Alderson

The only way to the top is by persistent, intelligent, hard work.

—A.T. Mercier

I realized early on that success was tied to not giving up. Most people in this business gave up and went on to other things. If you simply didn't give up, you would outlast the people who came in on the bus with you.

—Harrison Ford

The secret of success is constancy of purpose.

—Benjamin Disraeli

I'm hardnosed about luck. I think it sucks. Yeah, if you spend seven years looking for a job as a copywriter, and then one day somebody gives you a job, you can say, "Gee, I was lucky I happened to go up there today." But dammit, I was going to go up there sooner or later in the next seventy years.… If you're persistent in trying and doing and working, you almost make your own fortune.

—Jerry Della Femina

Flaming enthusiasm, backed up by horse sense and persistence, is the quality that most frequently makes for success.

—Dale Carnegie

It's the plugging away that will win you
    the day
So don't be a piker, old pard!
Just draw on your grit, it's so easy to
    quit—
It's the keeping your chin up that's hard.

—Robert W. Service

Be of good cheer. Do not think of today's failures, but of the success that may come tomorrow. You have set yourselves a difficult task, but you will succeed if you persevere; and you will find a joy in overcoming obstacles. Remember, no effort that we make to attain something beautiful is ever lost.

—Helen Keller

Perseverance is a great element of success. If you only knock long enough and loud enough at the gate, you are sure to wake up somebody.

—Henry Wadsworth Longfellow

Big shots are only little shots who keep shooting.

—Christopher Morley

Four steps to achievement: plan purposefully, prepare prayerfully, proceed positively, pursue persistently.

—William A. Ward

A winner never quits, and a quitter never wins.

—Unknown

Entrepreneurs average 3.8 failures before final success. What sets the successful ones apart is their amazing persistence. There are a lot of people out there with good and marketable ideas, but pure entrepreneurial types almost never accept defeat.

—Lisa M. Amos

The way to succeed is never quit. That's it. But really be humble about it.... You start out lowly and humble and you carefully try to learn an accretion of little things that help you get there.

—Alex Hailey

There are no shortcuts to any place worth going.

—Beverly Sills

Plodding wins the race.

—Aesop

No one succeeds without effort.... Those who succeed owe their success to their perseverance.

—Ramana Maharshi

The difficulties and struggles of today are but the price we must pay for the accomplishments and victories of tomorrow.

—William J.H. Boetcker

Men who have attained things worth having in this world have worked while others idled, have persevered when others gave up in despair, have practiced early in life the valuable habits of self-denial, industry, and singleness of purpose. As a result, they enjoy in later life the success so often erroneously attributed to good luck.

—Grenvill Kleiser

Continuous effort—not strength or intelligence—is the key to unlocking our potential.

—Sir Winston Churchill

Let me tell you the secret that has led me to my goal. My strength lies solely in my tenacity.

—Louis Pasteur

In the realm of ideas, everything depends on enthusiasm; in the real world, all rests on perseverance.

—Johann von Goethe

It isn't hard to be good from time to time in sports. What's tough is being good every day.

—Willie Mays

If you start to take Vienna, take Vienna.

—Napoleon Bonaparte

There's such a thin line between winning and losing.

—John R. Tunis

SUCCESS TAKES TIME

It takes time to be a success.

—Unknown

It takes twenty years to make an
overnight success.

—Eddie Cantor

Actually, I'm an overnight success. But it
took twenty years.

—Monty Hall

It takes time to succeed because success is
merely the natural reward for taking time
to do anything well.

—Joseph Ross

Success generally depends upon knowing
how long it takes to succeed.

—Charles de Montesquieu

Success Is Relative

Our business in life is not to get ahead of others but to get ahead of ourselves—to break our own records, to outstrip our yesterdays by our today, to do our work with more force than ever before.
> —Steward B. Johnson

Success is to be measured not so much by the position that one has reached in life as by the obstacles which he has overcome.
> —Booker T. Washington

Success has always been easy to measure. It is the distance between one's origins and one's final achievement.
> —Michael Korda

How can they say my life is not a success? Have I not for more than sixty years got enough to eat and escaped being eaten?
> —Logan Pearsall Smith

Success is relative: It is what we can make
of the mess we have made of things.

—T.S. Eliot

Survival is triumph enough.

—Harry Crews

The man who has done his level best,
and who is conscious that he has done
his best, is a success, even though the
world may write him down a failure.

—B.C. Forbes

Success is living up to your potential.
That's all. Wake up with a smile and go
after life…. Live it, enjoy it, taste it,
smell it, feel it.

—Joe Kapp

On earth we have nothing to do with
success or results, but only with being
true to God, and for God. Defeat in
doing right is nevertheless victory.

—E.W. Robertson

A successful man is he who receives a great deal from his fellow men, usually incomparably more than corresponds to his service to them. The value of a man, however, should be seen in what he gives, and not in what he is able to receive.

—Albert Einstein

The reward of a thing well done is to have done it.

—Ralph Waldo Emerson

The conventional army loses if it does not win. The guerrilla wins if he does not lose.

—Henry Kissinger

My success is measured by my willingness to keep trying.

—Unknown

If you've had a good time playing the game, you're a winner even if you lose.

—Malcolm Forbes

I have fought a good fight, I have fin-
ished my course, I have kept the faith.

—The Bible, II Timothy

Success is peace of mind, which is a
direct result of knowing you did your
best to become the best that you are
capable of becoming.

—John Wooden

I'd rather be a lamppost in Chicago than
a millionaire in any other city.

—William A. Hulbert

SUCCESS IS DOING WHAT'S RIGHT FOR US

There is only one success—to be able to spend your life in your own way.
                              —Christopher Morley

The only success worth one's powder was success in the line of one's idiosyncrasy … what was talent but the art of being completely whatever one happened to be?
                              —Henry James

We only do well the things we like doing.
                              —Colette

Success based on anything but internal fulfillment is bound to be empty.
                              —Dr. Martha Friedman

Nature magically suits a man to his fortunes, by making them the fruit of his character.
                              —Ralph Waldo Emerson

All I would tell people is to hold on to
what was individual about themselves,
not to allow their ambition for success to
cause them to try to imitate the success
of others. You've got to find it on your
own terms.

—Harrison Ford

For me, writing is the only thing that
passes the three tests of *metier:* (1) when
I'm doing it, I don't feel that I should be
doing something else instead; (2) it produces a sense of accomplishment and,
once in a while, pride; and (3) it's
frightening.

—Gloria Steinem

One can never consent to creep when
one feels an impulse to soar.

—Helen Keller

A first-rate soup is better than a second-
rate painting.

—Abraham Maslow

My mother said to me, "If you become a soldier, you'll be a general, if you become a monk you'll end up as the pope." Instead, I became a painter and wound up as Picasso.

—Pablo Picasso

Abasement, degradation is simply the manner of life of the man who has refused to be what it is his duty to be.

—Jose Ortega y Gasset

Different people have different duties assigned to them by Nature; Nature has given one the power or the desire to do this, the other that. Each bird must sing with his own throat.

—Henrik Ibsen

We succeed in enterprises which demand the positive qualities we possess, but we excel in those which can also make use of our defects.

—Alexis de Tocqueville

We can't all be heroes because someone has to sit on the curb and clap as they go by.
—Will Rogers

I'd rather be a lamppost in Chicago than a millionaire in any other city.
—William A. Hulbert

A man can do only what he can do. But if he does that each day he can sleep at night and do it again the next day.
—Albert Schweitzer

Don't take anyone else's definition of success as your own. (This is easier said than done.)
—Jacqueline Briskin

Whatever you are by nature, keep to it; never desert your own line of talent. Be what nature intended you for, and you will succeed; be anything else and you will be ten thousand times worse than nothing.
—Sydney Smith

Ask yourself the secret of *your* success.
Listen to your answer, and practice it.
—Richard Bach

I cannot do everything, but still I can
do something; and because I cannot do
everything I will not refuse to do
something that I can do.
—Edward E. Hale

Starting out to make money is the
greatest mistake in life. Do what you feel
you have a flair for doing, and if you are
good enough at it, the money will come.
—Greer Garson

If a man has a talent and cannot use it,
he has failed. If he has a talent and uses
only half of it, he has partly failed. If he
has a talent and learns somehow to use
the whole of it, he has gloriously
succeeded, and won a satisfaction and a
triumph few men ever know.
—Thomas Wolfe

BEFORE WE CAN SUCCEED, WE HAVE TO NOT FAIL

Most ball games are lost, not won.
                                        —Casey Stengel

Before you can win a game, you have to not lose it.
                                        —Chuck Noll

Football games aren't won, they're lost.
                                        —Fielding Yost

THE JOURNEY IS MORE IMPORTANT THAN ARRIVING

Success is a journey, not a destination.
—Ben Sweetland

It is good to have an end to journey toward; but it is the journey that matters, in the end.
—Ursula K. LeGuin

To live only for some future goal is shallow. It's the sides of the mountain that sustain life, not the top.
—Robert M. Pirsig

The reward of the general is not a bigger tent, but command.
—Oliver Wendell Holmes Jr.

In the long run, the pessimist may be proved to be right, but the optimist has a better time on the trip.
—Daniel L. Reardon

To travel hopefully is a better thing than
to arrive, and the true success is to labor.
—Robert Louis Stevenson

Despite the success cult, men are most
deeply moved not by the reaching of the
goal, but by the grandness of effort
involved in getting there—or failing to
get there.

—Max Lerner

We're still not where we're going, but
we're not where we were.
—Natash Jasefowitz

'Tis the motive exalts the action,
'Tis the doing, and not the deed.
—Margaret Junkin Preston

The problem is not that you cannot have
what you think you want. The problem
is that when you get what you think you
want, it won't satisfy.

—Unknown

Arriving at one goal is the starting point
to another.

—John Dewey

I think that wherever your journey takes
you, there are new gods waiting there,
with divine patience—and laughter.

—Susan M. Watkins

It has never been, and never will be, easy
work! But the road that is built in hope
is more pleasant to the traveler than the
road built in despair, even though they
both lead to the same destination.

—Marian Zimmer Bradley

The excursion is the same when you go
looking for your sorrow as when you go
looking for your joy.

—Eudora Welty

The reward of a thing well done is to
have done it.

—Ralph Waldo Emerson

We should scarcely desire things ardently
if we were perfectly acquainted with what
we desire.
>   —Francois de La Rochefoucauld

With the catching ends the pleasures of
the chase.
>   —Abraham Lincoln

To have realized your dream makes you
feel lost.
>   —Oriana Fallaci

We spend our time searching for security,
and hate it when we get it.
>   —John Steinbeck

The struggle alone pleases us, not the
victory.
>   —Blaise Pascal

Happiness is not a station to arrive at,
but a manner of traveling.
>   —Margaret Lee Runbeck

Happiness is to be found along the way, not at the end of the road, for then the journey is over and it is too late.

—Robert R. Updegraff

Need and struggle are what excite and inspire us; our hour of triumph is what brings the void.

—William James

The really happy man is one who can enjoy the scenery on a detour.

—Unknown

You wear yourself out in the pursuit of wealth or love or freedom, you do everything to gain some right, and once it's gained you take no pleasure in it.

—Oriana Fallaci

SUCCESS ISN'T THE TOTAL ANSWER

Success is counted sweetest by those who
ne'er succeed.

—Emily Dickinson

Success has ruined many a man.

—Benjamin Franklin

Granting our wish is one of Fate's saddest
jokes.

—James Russell Lowell

Now that I'm here, where am I?

—Janis Joplin

Success is not greedy, as people think,
but insignificant. That's why it satisfies
nobody.

—Marcus Annaeus Seneca

Is there anything in life so disenchanting
as attainment?

—Robert Louis Stevenson

Nothing fails like success; nothing is so
defeated as yesterday's triumphant cause.
—Phyllis McGinley

There are two tragedies in life. One is to
lose your heart's desire. The other is to
gain it.
—George Bernard Shaw

Fame always brings loneliness. Success is
as ice cold and lonely as the North Pole.
—Vicki Baum

Success has killed more men than bullets.
—Texas Guinan

Achievement: The death of an endeavor,
and the birth of disgust.
—Ambrose Bierce

The problems of victory are more agree-
able than those of defeat, but they are no
less difficult.
—Sir Winston Churchill

Success and failure are equally disastrous.
—Tennessee Williams

We are never further from our wishes
than when we imagine that we possess
what we have desired.
—Johann von Goethe

Some aspects of success seem rather silly
as death approaches.
—Donald A. Miller

If I had known what it would be like to
have it all, I might have been willing to
settle for less.
—Lily Tomlin

Success and failure are both difficult to
endure. Along with success come drugs,
divorce, fornication, bullying, travel,
meditation, medication, depression,
neurosis and suicide. With failure comes
failure.
—Joseph Heller

Unless a man has been taught what to do with success after getting it, the achievement of it must inevitably leave him a prey to boredom.

—Bertrand Russell

The two hardest things to handle in life are failure and success.

—Unknown

The best thing that can come with success is the knowledge that it is nothing to long for.

—Liv Ullmann

The closer one gets to the top, the more one finds there is no "top."

—Nancy Barcus

The toughest thing about success is that you've got to keep on being a success. Talent is only a starting point in business. You've got to keep working that talent.

—Irving Berlin

Oh, how quickly the world's glory passes away.

—Thomas a'Kempis

The minute you think you've got it made, disaster is just around the corner.

—Joe Paterno

Creating success is tough. But keeping it is tougher. You have to keep producing, you can't ever stop.

—Pete Rose

We would often be sorry if our wishes were gratified.

—Aesop

Nothing except a battle lost can be half so melancholy as a battle won.

—Arthur Wellesley, Duke of Wellington

We grow weary of those things (and perhaps soonest) which we most desire.

—Samuel Butler

Our desires always increase with our possessions. The knowledge that something remains yet unenjoyed impairs our enjoyment of the good before us.

—Samuel Johnson

The prospect of success in achieving our most cherished dream is not without its terrors. Who is more deprived and alone than the man who has achieved his dream?

—Brendan Francis

Oddly enough, success over a period of time is more expensive than failure.

—Grant Tinker

There must be more to life than having everything!

—Maurice Sendak

Being frustrated is disagreeable, but the real disasters of life begin when you get what you want.

—Irving Kristol

If you live long enough, you'll see that
every victory turns into a defeat.
> —Simone de Beauvoir

Out of every fruition of success, no matter what, comes forth something to make
a new effort necessary.
> —Walt Whitman

It's not that I'm not grateful for all this
attention. It's just that fame and fortune
ought to add up to more than fame and
fortune.
> —Robert Fulghum

Adversity is sometimes hard upon a man,
but for one man who can stand prosperi-
ty, there are a hundred that will stand
adversity.
> —Thomas Carlyle

One more such victory and we are
undone.
> —Pyrrhus

Pray that success will not come any faster
than you are able to endure it.

—Elbert Hubbard

Success can also cause misery. The trick is
not to be surprised when you discover it
doesn't bring you all the happiness and
answers you thought it would.

—Prince

Other Definitions of Success

Success is getting what you want; happiness is wanting what you get.

— Unknown

Life is a succession of moments. To live each one is to succeed.

— Corita Kent

To laugh often and much;
To win the respect of intelligent people,
  and the affection of children;
To earn the appreciation of honest critics,
  and endure the betrayal of false friends;
To appreciate beauty;
To find the best in others;
To leave the world a bit better, whether
  by a healthy child, a garden patch, or a
  redeemed social condition;
To know that even one life has breathed
  easier because you lived.
This is to have succeeded.

— Ralph Waldo Emerson

Success has nothing to do with what you gain in life or accomplish for yourself. It's what you do for others.

—Danny Thomas

If you have a good name, if you are right more often than you are wrong, if your children respect you, if your grandchildren are glad to see you, if your friends can count on you and you can count on them in time of trouble, if you can face your God and say "I have done my best," then you are a success.

—Ann Landers

You have reached the pinnacle of success as soon as you become uninterested in money, compliments, or publicity.

—Thomas Wolfe

GENERAL QUOTATIONS ABOUT SUCCESS

Marconi invented radio, but Ted Husing knew what to do with it.

—Ralph Edwards

Success produces success, just as money produces money.

—Nicholas de Chamfort

God may allow His servant to succeed when He has disciplined him to a point where he does not need to succeed to be happy. The man who is elated by success and is cast down by failure is still a carnal man. At best his fruit will have a worm in it.

—A.W. Tozer

There is no business in the world so troublesome as the pursuit of fame: life is over before you have hardly begun your work.

—Jean de La Bruyere

Nothing fails like success because we don't
learn from it. We learn only from failure.
—Kenneth Boudling

All outward success, when it has value, is
but the inevitable result of an inward
success of full living, full play and enjoyment of one's faculties.
—Robert Henri

There are three types of baseball play-
ers—those who make it happen, those
who watch it happen, and those who
wonder what happened.
—Tommy Lasorda

The exclusive worship of the bitch-
goddess Success is our national disease.
—William James

I have found that it is much easier to
make a success in life than to make a
success of one's life.
—G.W. Follin

Success causes us to be more praised than known.

—Joseph Roux

Along with success comes a reputation for wisdom.

—Euripides

Great men have not been concerned with fame. The joy of achievement that comes from finding something new in the universe is by far their greatest joy.

—William P. King

Out of the strain of the Doing, into the peace of the Done.

—Julia Louise Woodruff

Success is like a liberation, or the first phase of a love affair.

—Jeanne Moreau

There is always room at the top.

—Daniel Webster

Success makes men rigid and they tend
to exalt stability over all the other virtues;
tired of the effort of willing, they become
fanatics about conservatism.

—Walter Lippman

An act of love that fails is just as much a
part of the divine life as an act of love
that succeeds, for love is measured by its
own fullness, not by its reception.

—Harold Loukes

The best place to succeed is where you
are with what you have.

—Charles M. Schwab

Success covers a multitude of blunders.

—George Bernard Shaw

Victory at all costs, victory in spite of all
terror, victory however long and hard the
hard may be; for without victory there is
no survival.

—Sir Winston Churchill

How to succeed: try hard enough. How to fail: Try too hard.

—Malcolm Forbes

There could be no honor in a sure success, but much might be wrested from a sure defeat.

—T.E. Lawrence (Lawrence of Arabia)

Bad will be the day for every man when he becomes absolutely contented with the life he is living, when there is not forever beating at the doors of his soul some great desire to do something larger.

—Phillips Brooks

When there is no feeling of accomplishment, children fail to develop properly and old people rapidly decline.

—Joseph Whitney

Theirs is not to reason why, theirs is but to do or die.

—Alfred, Lord Tennyson

Those who have easy, cheerful attitudes tend to be happier than those with less pleasant temperaments, regardless of money, "making it," or success.

—Dr. Joyce Brothers

In war there is no second prize for the runner-up.

—General Omar N. Bradley

PART TWO

LUCK

LUCK CAN BE VERY IMPORTANT

Luck is everything…. My good luck in
life was to be a really frightened person.
I'm fortunate to be a coward, to have a
low threshold of fear, because a hero
couldn't make a good suspense film.

—Alfred Hitchcock

I would rather have a lucky general than
a smart general…. They win battles, and
they make me lucky.

—Dwight D. Eisenhower

Everything in life is luck.

—Donald Trump

'Tis man's to fight, but Heaven's to give
success.

—Homer

I am persuaded that luck and timing
have, in my case, been very important.

—Mike Wallace

I have been extraordinarily lucky. Anyone who pretends that some kind of luck isn't involved in his success is deluding himself.
—Arthur Hailey

In the queer mess of human destiny, the determining factor is luck.
—William E. Woodward

I wish I could tell you that the Children's Television Workshop and Sesame Street were thanks to my genius, but it really was a lucky break.
—Joan Ganz Cooney

No writer should minimize the factor that affects everyone, but is beyond control: luck.
—John Jakes

Though men pride themselves on their great actions, often they are not the result of any great design, but of chance.
—Francois de La Rochefoucauld

'Tis better to be fortunate than wise.
—John Webster

Much of my good fortune was a matter
of nothing more clever on my part than
luck.
—James Fixx

Everything that happened to me hap-
pened by mistake. I don't believe in fate.
It's luck, timing and accident.
—Merv Griffin

Name the greatest of all inventors:
Accident.
—Mark Twain

Still, We Can't Depend Too Heavily on Luck

Luck always seems to be against the man who depends on it.

—Unknown

Good luck is often with the man who doesn't include it in his plans.

—Unknown

Depend on the rabbit's foot if you will, but it didn't work for the rabbit!

—Unknown

The worst cynicism, a belief in luck.

—Joyce Carol Oates

Destiny is the invention of the cowardly, and the resigned.

—Ignazio Silone

Luck is what a capricious man believes in.

—Benjamin Disraeli

Luck serves … as rationalization for
every people that is not master of its own
destiny.

—Hannah Arendt

They who await no gifts from chance
have conquered fate.

—Matthew Arnold

To believe in luck … is skepticism.

—Ralph Waldo Emerson

Shallow men believe in luck, wise and
strong men in cause and effect.

—Ralph Waldo Emerson

Those who trust to chance must abide by
the results of chance.

—Calvin Coolidge

It is a madness to make fortune the
mistress of events, because in herself she
is nothing, but is ruled by prudence.

—John Dryden

Luck is a word devoid of sense; nothing can exist without a cause.

—Voltaire

Woe to him who would ascribe something like reason to Chance, and make a religion of surrendering to it.

—Johann von Goethe

Fortune is the rod of the weak, and the staff of the brave.

—James Russell Lowell

The man who is intent on making the most of his opportunities is too busy to bother about luck.

—B.C. Forbes

Luck implies an absolute absence of any principle.

—Chuang-tzu

WE MUST CREATE OUR OWN LUCK

I'm hardnosed about luck. I think it sucks. Yeah, if you spend seven years looking for a job as a copywriter, and then one day somebody gives you a job, you can say, "Gee, I was lucky I happened to go up there today." But dammit, I was going to go up there sooner or later in the next seventy years.... If you're persistent in trying and doing and working, you almost make your own fortune.

—Jerry Della Femina

It is a great piece of skill to know how to guide your luck, even while waiting for it.

—Baltasar Gracian

I was thinking of my patients, and how the worst moment for them was when they discovered they were masters of bad or good luck. When they could no longer blame fate, they were in despair.

—Anais Nin

Some are satisfied to stand politely before the portals of Fortune and to await her bidding; better those who push forward, who employ their enterprise, who on the wings of their worth and valor seek to embrace luck, and to effectively gain her favor.

—Baltasar Gracian

The champion makes his own luck.

—Red Blaik

You don't just luck into things.... You build step by step, whether it's friendships or opportunities.

—Barbara Bush

Failure and success seem to have been allotted to men by their stars. But they retain the power of wriggling, of fighting with their star or against it, and in the whole universe the only really interesting movement is this wriggle.

—E.M. Forster

Chance never helps those who do not
help themselves.

—Sophocles

If fate means you to lose, give him a
good fight anyhow.

—William McFee

Go and wake up your luck.

—Persian proverb

We create our fate every day.… Most of
the ills we suffer from are directly
traceable to our own behavior.

—Henry Miller

Of course, fortune has its part in human
affairs, but conduct is really much more
important.

—Jeanne Detourbey

We must master our good fortune, or it
will master us.

—Publilius Syrus

Good Luck Comes from Hard Work

I'm a great believer in luck, and I find
the harder I work, the more I have of it.
—Thomas Jefferson

Luck means the hardships and privations
which you have not hesitated to endure,
the long nights you have devoted to
work. Luck means the appointments you
have never failed to keep, the trains you
have never failed to catch.
—Max O'Relling

Luck is what you have left over after you
give 100 percent.
—Langston Coleman

Luck is not chance, it's toil; fortune's
expensive smile is earned.
—Emily Dickinson

I find I'm luckier when I work harder.
—Dr. Denton Cooley

The lucky fellow is the plucky fellow
who has been burning midnight oil and
taking defeat after defeat with a smile.
—James B. Hill

Men who have attained things worth
having in this world have worked while
others idled, have persevered when others
gave up in despair, have practiced early in
life the valuable habits of self-denial, industry, and singleness of purpose. As a result,
they enjoy in later life the success so often
erroneously attributed to good luck.
—Grenville Kleiser

Luck is the by-product of busting your fanny.
—Don Sutton

When you work seven days a week,
fourteen hours a day, you get lucky.
—Armand Hammer

Chance favors those in motion.
—Dr. James H. Austin

No man ever wetted clay and then left it, as if
there would be bricks by chance and fortune.
—Plutarch

It's hard to detect good luck—it looks so
much like something you've earned.
—Frank A. Clark

Work and acquire, and thou hast chained
the wheel of Chance.
—Ralph Waldo Emerson

Superiority to fate is difficult to gain, 'tis
not conferred of any, but possible to earn.
—Emily Dickinson

Some folk want their luck buttered.
—Thomas Hardy

Diligence is the mother of good luck,
and God gives all things to industry.
—Benjamin Franklin

Fortune is ever seen accompanying industry.
—Oliver Goldsmith

BOLDNESS AND COURAGE CAN HELP CREATE LUCK

Fortune favours the bold.

—Terence

A stout heart breaks bad luck.

—Miguel de Cervantes

Fortune reveres the brave, and
overwhelms the cowardly.

—Marcus Annaeus Seneca

Fortune sides with him who dares.

—Virgil

WE MUST PREPARE FOR LUCK

Chance favors the prepared mind.
—Louis Pasteur

You have to be eligible for luck to strike, and I think that's a matter of education and preparation, and character and all the other solid attributes that sometimes people laugh at.
—James A. Michener

Get as much experience as you can, so that you're ready when luck works. That's the luck.
—Henry Fonda

Chance does nothing that has not been prepared beforehand.
—Alexis de Tocqueville

Combine common sense and the Golden Rule, and you will have very little bad luck.
—Unknown

You've got to be in a position for luck to happen. Luck doesn't go around looking for a stumblebum.

—Darrell Royal

Luck is the residue of design.

—Branch Rickey

Luck affects everything. Let your hook be always cast. In the stream where you least expect it, there will be fish.

—Ovid

Luck is being ready for the chance.

—J. Frank Dobie

Chance usually favors the prudent man.

—Joseph Joubert

Thorough preparation makes its own luck.

—Joe Poyer

Luck is a matter of preparation meeting opportunity.

—Oprah Winfrey

WE MUST RECOGNIZE AND
MAXIMIZE OUR LUCK

There are so many people with all kinds
of lucky things happening to them, and
they don't know how to use it.

—Rocky Aoki

Probably any successful career has "X"
number of breaks in it, and maybe the
difference between successful people and
those who aren't superachievers is taking
advantage of those breaks.

—Joan Ganz Cooney

It's funny, but … you're sort of a moving
target for fortune, and you never know
when it will befall you.

—Thomas McGuane

Luck … taps, once in a lifetime, at everybody's door, but if industry does not
open it, luck goes away.

—Charles Haddon Spurgeon

You must always be open to your luck. You cannot force it, but you can recognize it.

—Henry Moore

When something bad happens to me, I think I'm able to deal with it in a pretty good way. That makes me lucky. Some people fall apart at the first little thing that happens.

—Christie Brinkley

A wise man turns chance into good fortune.

—Thomas Fuller

OTHER SOURCES OF LUCK

Lady Luck generally woos those who earnestly, enthusiastically, unremittingly woo her.

—B.C. Forbes

Luck is good planning, carefully executed.

—Unknown

What helps luck is a habit of watching for opportunities, of having a patient, but restless mind, of sacrificing one's ease or vanity, of uniting a love of detail to foresight, and of passing through hard times bravely and cheerfully.

—Charles Victor Cherbuliez

Luck is believing you're lucky.

—Tennessee Williams

I think that one can have luck if one tries to create an atmosphere of spontaneity.

—Federico Fellini

Each man's character shapes his fortunes.
—Latin proverb

Chance works for us when we are good captains.
—George Meredith

Motivation triggers luck.
—Mike Wallace

Good and bad luck is a synonym, in the great majority of instances, for good and bad judgment.
—John Chatfield

Luck is largely a matter of paying attention.
—Susan M. Dodd

Your luck is how you treat people.
—Bridget O'Donnell

Luck is a combination of confidence and getting the breaks.
—Christy Mathewson

LUCK CHANGES

The only sure thing about luck is that it will change.

—Bret Harte

The profits of good luck are perishable; if you build on fortune, you build on sand; the more advancement you achieve, the more dangers you run.

—Marquis de Racan

The man who glories in his luck may be overthrown by destiny.

—Euripides

There is in the worst of fortune the best of chances for a happy change.

—Euripides

What the reason of the ant laboriously drags into a heap, the wind of accident will collect in one breath.

—J.C.F. von Schiller

Life is full of chances and changes, and the most prosperous of men may ... meet with great misfortunes.

—Aristotle

Every possession and every happiness is but lent by chance for an uncertain time, and may therefore be demanded back the next hour.

—Arthur Schopenhauer

Fortune is like the market, where many times, if you can stay a little, the price will fall.

—Francis Bacon

Fortune is with you for an hour, and against you for ten!

—Arab proverb

Breaks balance out. The sun don't shine on the same old dog's rear end every day.

—Darrell Royal

PART THREE

OPPORTUNITY

LIFE IS FULL OF OPPORTUNITIES, BUT WE OFTEN MISS THEM

Great opportunities come to all, but many do not know they have met them. The only preparation to take advantage of them is simple fidelity to watch what each day brings.

—Albert E. Dunning

The world is all gates, all opportunities, strings of tension waiting to be struck.

—Ralph Waldo Emerson

Do not wait for ideal circumstances, nor for the best opportunities; they will never come.

—Janet Erskine Stuart

Men do with opportunities as children do at the seashore; they fill their little hands with sand, and then let the grains fall through, one by one, till all are gone.

—T. Jones

No great man ever complains of want of opportunity.

—Ralph Waldo Emerson

Nothing is so often irretrievably missed as a daily opportunity.

—Marie von Ebner-Eschenbach

If a man looks sharply and attentively, he shall see fortune; for though she be blind, yet she is not invisible.

—Francis Bacon

Know thine opportunity.

—Pittacus

In great affairs we ought to apply ourselves less to creating chances than to profiting from those that are offered.

—Francois de La Rochefoucauld

Opportunity is as scarce as oxygen; men fairly breathe it and do not know it.

—Doc Sane

Opportunities do not come with their values stamped upon them…. To face every opportunity of life thoughtfully, and ask its meaning bravely and earnestly, is the only way to meet supreme opportunities when they come, whether open-faced or disguised.

—Maltbie D. Babcock

We are told that talent creates its own opportunities. But it sometimes seems that intense desire creates not only its own opportunities, but its own talents.

—Eric Hoffer

How many opportunities present themselves to a man without his noticing them?

—Arab proverb

Luck affects everything. Let your hook be always cast. In the stream where you least expect it, there will be a fish.

—Ovid

The opportunity that God sends does
not wake up him who is asleep.
—Senegalese proverb

Present opportunities are neglected, and
attainable good is slighted, by minds
busied in extensive ranges and intent
upon future advantages.
—Samuel Johnson

The opportunities for enjoyment in your
life are limitless. If you feel you are not
experiencing enough joy, you have only
yourself to blame.
—David E. Bresler

Opportunities multiply as they are
seized; they die when neglected. Life is a
long line of opportunities.
—John Wicker

Opportunities are often things you
haven't noticed the first time around.
—Catherine Deneuve

I think luck is the sense to recognize an opportunity and the ability to take advantage of it. Everyone has bad breaks, but everyone also has opportunities. The man who can smile at his breaks and grab his chances gets on.

—Samuel Goldwyn

To improve the golden moment of opportunity, and catch the good that is within our reach, is the great art of life.

—Samuel Johnson

The greatest achievement of the human spirit is to live up to one's opportunities, and make the most of one's resources.

—Vauvenargues

Opportunity knocks but once.

—Unknown

What the student calls a tragedy, the master calls a butterfly.

—Richard Bach

But we often look so long and so regret-
fully upon the closed door that we do
not see the one which has opened for us.
—Helen Keller

It is often hard to distinguish between
the hard knocks in life and those of
opportunity.
—Frederick Phillips

If Fortune calls, offer him a seat.
—Yiddish proverb

I was seldom able to see an opportunity
until it had ceased to be one.
—Mark Twain

Vigilance in watching opportunity; tact
and daring in seizing upon opportunity;
force and persistence in crowding
opportunity to its utmost possible
achievement—these are the martial
virtues which must command success.
—Austin Phelps

To avoid an occasion for our virtues is a worse degree of failure than to push forward pluckily and make a fall.

—Robert Louis Stevenson

When one door closes, another opens. The successful man is one who had the chance and took it.

—Roger Babson

Opportunity is missed by most people because it is dressed in overalls, and looks like work.

—Thomas A. Edison

OPPORTUNITIES ARE OFTEN FOUND IN TOUGH SITUATIONS

Times of stress and difficulty are seasons of opportunity when the seeds of progress are sown.

—Thomas F. Woodlock

We must look for the opportunity in every difficulty instead of being paralyzed at the thought of the difficulty in every opportunity.

—Walter E. Cole

WE MUST PREPARE FOR OUR OPPORTUNITIES

The secret to success in life is for a man to be ready for his opportunity when it comes.
—Benjamin Disraeli

I think the young actor who really wants to act will find a way … to keep at it and seize every opportunity that comes along.
—Sir John Gielgud

Unless a man has trained himself for his chance, the chance will only make him ridiculous.
—William Matthews

Opportunity rarely knocks until you are ready. And few people have ever been really ready without receiving opportunity's call.
—Channing Pollock

Opportunity can benefit no man who has not fitted himself to seize it and use it. Opportunity woos the worthy, shuns the unworthy. Prepare yourself to grasp opportunity, and opportunity is likely to come your way. It is not so fickle, capricious and unreasoning as some complain.

—B.C. Forbes

We Must Also Create Our Own Opportunities

A wise man will make more opportunities than he finds.

—Francis Bacon

Mediocre men wait for opportunity to come to them. Strong, able, alert men go after opportunity.

—B.C. Forbes

You don't just luck into things ... you build step by step, whether it's friendships or opportunities.

—Barbara Bush

Every man is the architect of his own fortune.

—Sallust

If you want to succeed in the world, you must make your own opportunities.

—John B. Gough

Many things are lost for want of asking.
                    —English proverb

A filly who wants to run will always find
a rider.

                    —Jacques Audiberti

He that waits upon fortune is never sure
of a dinner.

                    —Benjamin Franklin

OPPORTUNITY AND SECURITY

There is no security on this earth. Only opportunity.
—General Douglas MacArthur

Too many people are thinking of security instead of opportunity; they seem more afraid of life than of death.
—James F. Byrnes

Freedom is nothing else but a chance to be better, whereas enslavement is a certainty of the worst.
—Albert Camus

WE OFTEN LOSE OPPORTUNITIES BY OVERDELIBERATION

The opportunity is often lost by deliberating.

—Publilius Syrus

You decide you'll wait for your pitch. Then as the ball starts toward the plate, you think about your stance. And then you think about your swing. And then you realize that the ball that went past you for a strike was your pitch.

—Bobby Murcer

General Quotations about Opportunity

Small opportunities are often the beginning of great enterprises.

—Demosthenes

The follies which a man regrets most in his life are those which he didn't commit when he had the opportunity.

—Helen Rowland

Ability is of little account without opportunity.

—Napoleon Bonaparte

Our opportunities to do good are our talents.

—Cotton Mather

A door that seems to stand open must be a man's size, or it is not the door that Providence means for him.

—Henry Ward Beecher

Next to knowing when to seize an opportunity, the most important thing in life is to know when to forgo an advantage.
—Benjamin Disraeli

Opportunity knocks at every man's door once. On some men's door it hammers till it breaks down the door and then it goes in and wakes him up if he's asleep, and ever afterward it works for him as a night watchman.
—Finley Peter Dunne

It is less important to redistribute wealth than it is to redistribute opportunity.
—Arthur Vandenberg

It is not manly to turn one's back on fortune.
—Marcus Annaeus Seneca

PART FOUR

COMMITMENT

To Live Fully and Successfully, We Must Commit to Something

If you don't make a total commitment to whatever you're doing, then you start looking to bail out the first time the boat starts leaking. It's tough enough getting that boat to shore with everybody rowing, let alone when a guy stands up and starts putting his life jacket on.

—Lou Holtz

If a man hasn't discovered something that he will die for, he isn't fit to live.

—Martin Luther King Jr.

Winners are men who have dedicated their whole lives to winning.

—Woody Hayes

Unless you can find some sort of loyalty, you cannot find unity and peace in your active living.

—Josiah Royce

Sometimes success is due less to ability than zeal. The winner is he who gives himself to his work body and soul.
—Charles Buxton

Now I am steel-set: I follow the call to the clear radiance and glow of the heights.
—Henrik Ibsen

Love me, please, I love you; I can bear to be your friend. So ask of me anything.... I am not a tentative person. Whatever I do, I give up my whole self to it.
—Edna Saint Vincent Millay

I don't care a damn for your loyal service when you think I am right; when I really want it most is when you think I am wrong.
—General Sir John Monash

If you don't stand for something, you'll fall for anything.
—Michael Evans

One's lifework, I have learned, grows
with the working and the living. Do it as
if your life depended on it, and first
thing you know, you'll have made a life
out of it. A good life, too.

—Theresa Helburn

If you deny yourself commitment, what
can you do with your life?

—Harvey Fierstein

The person who makes a success of living
is the one who sees his goal steadily and
aims for it unswervingly. That is dedication.

—Cecil B. DeMille

Theirs is not to reason why, theirs is but
to do or die.

—Alfred, Lord Tennyson

Put your heart, mind, intellect and soul
even to your smallest acts. This is the
secret of success.

—Swami Sivananda

Either do not attempt at all, or go
through with it.

—Ovid

If you start to take Vienna, take Vienna.
—Napoleon Bonaparte

If you aren't going all the way, why go at all?
—Joe Namath

You can be an ordinary athlete by getting
away with less than your best. But if you
want to be a great, you have to give it all
you've got—your everything.
—Duke P. Kahanamoku

Men, like snails, lose their usefulness when
they lose direction and begin to bend.
—Walter Savage Landor

It is by losing himself in the objective, in
inquiry, creation, and craft, that a man
becomes something.
—Paul Goodman

It is fatal to enter any war without the will to win it.
—General Douglas MacArthur

Moderation in war is imbecility.
—Admiral John Fisher

The height of your accomplishments will equal the depth of your convictions.
—William F. Scolavino

The dedicated life is the life worth living.
—Annie Dillard

The secret of living is to find a pivot, the pivot of a concept on which you can make your stand.
—Luigi Pirandello

The Perils of the Middle of the Road

There's nothing in the middle of the road
but yellow stripes and dead armadillos.
                                    —Jim Hightower

Standing in the middle of the road is
very dangerous; you get knocked down
by traffic from both sides.
                                    —Margaret Thatcher

He who walks in the middle of the road
gets hit from both sides.
                                    —George P. Schultz

I never liked the middle ground—the
most boring place in the world.
                                    —Louise Nevelson

The hottest places in hell are reserved for
those who, in a period of moral crisis,
maintain their neutrality.
                                    —Dante Alighieri

The man who sees both sides of an issue
is very likely on the fence or up a tree.
—Unknown

The principle of neutrality … has increas-
ingly become an obsolete conception, and,
except under very special circumstances, it
is an immoral and shortsighted conception.
—John Foster Dulles

We know what happens to people who
stay in the middle of the road. They get
run over.
—Aneurin Bevan

The middle of the road is where the white
line is, and that's the worst place to drive.
—Robert Frost

Show me a person who is not an extrem-
ist about some things, who is a "middle-
of-the-roader" in everything, and I will
show you someone who is insecure.
—G. Aiken Taylor

INDIFFERENCE

There is nothing harder than the softness
of indifference.

> —Juan Montalvo

The opposite of love is not hate, it's
    indifference.
The opposite of art is not ugliness, it's
    indifference.
The opposite of faith is not heresy, it's
    indifference.
And the opposite of life is not death, it's
    indifference.

> —Elie Wiesel

COMMITMENT AND THE HEART

The only place you can win a football game is on the field. The only place you can lose it is in your heart.

—Darrell Royal

I am seeking, I am striving, I am in it with all my heart.

—Vincent van Gogh

Wars may be fought with weapons, but they are won by men. It is the spirit of the men who follow, and of the man who leads, that gains the victory.

—General George S. Patton

It was my tongue that swore; my heart is unsworn.

—Euripides

Morale is the greatest single factor in successful wars.

—Dwight D. Eisenhower

COMMITMENT AND WILLPOWER

Nothing can resist a will which will stake
even existence upon its fulfillment.
—Benjamin Disraeli

Your own resolution to success is more
important than any other one thing.
—Abraham Lincoln

The will to conquer is the first condition
of victory.
—Marshal Ferdinand Foch

Our future and our fate lie in our wills
more than in our hands, for our hands
are but the instruments of our wills.
—B.C. Forbes

Nothing is so common as unsuccessful
men with talent. They lack only
determination.
—Charles Swindoll

Strength is a matter of the made-up mind.
                                    —John Beecher

Nothing is difficult to those who have
the will.
        —Motto of the Dutch Poets' Society

COMMITMENT AND BELIEF

What distinguishes the majority of men
from the few is their ability to act
accordingly to their beliefs.

—Henry Miller

When you have decided what you believe,
what you feel must be done, have the
courage to stand alone and be counted.

—Eleanor Roosevelt

What a man believes, he will die for.
What a man merely thinks, he will
change his mind about.

—Unknown

Whether you are really right or not
doesn't matter, it's the belief that counts.

—Robertson Davies

A belief which does not spring from a conviction in the emotions is no belief at all.

—Evelyn Scott

The eloquent man is he who is no beautiful speaker, but who is inwardly and desperately drunk with a certain belief.

—Ralph Waldo Emerson

SOMETIMES WE MUST BURN OUR BRIDGES BEHIND US

Many a man has walked up to the opportunity for which he has long been preparing himself, looked it full in the face, and then begun to get cold feet … when it comes to betting on yourself and your power to do the thing you know you must do or write yourself down a failure, you're a chicken-livered coward if you hesitate.

—B.C. Forbes

Anytime you play golf for whatever you've got, that's pressure. I'd like to see H.L. Hunt go out there and play for $3 billion.

—Lee Trevino

Poverty is uncomfortable, as I can testify: but nine times out of ten the best thing that can happen to a young man is to be tossed overboard and compelled to sink or swim for himself.

—James A. Garfield

The wise man puts all his eggs in one basket and watches the basket.
                                    —Andrew Carnegie

There is a point at which everything becomes simple and there is no longer any question of choice, because all you have staked will be lost if you look back. Life's point of no return.
                                    —Dag Hammarskjold

Even now we can draw back. But once we cross that little bridge, we must settle things by the sword.
        —Julius Caesar, to his troops as they
            prepared to cross the Rubicon River

You don't know what pressure is until you play for $5 with only $2 in your pocket.
                                    —Lee Trevino

The fixed determination to have acquired the warrior soul, to either conquer or perish with honor, is the secret of victory.
                                    —General George S. Patton

COMMITMENT AND WARFARE

In war there is no substitute for victory.
—Dwight D. Eisenhower

Victory at all costs, victory in spite of all terror, victory however long and hard the road may be; for without victory there is no survival.

—Sir Winston Churchill

Better that we should die fighting than be outraged and dishonored. Better to die than to live in slavery.
—Emmeline Pankhurst

I sincerely wish war was a pleasanter and easier business than it is, but it does not admit of holidays.
—Abraham Lincoln

Every attempt to make war easy and safe will result in humiliation and disaster.
—General William Sherman

General Quotations about Commitment

The worth of every conviction consists precisely in the steadfastness with which it is held.

—Jane Adams

The moment one definitely commits oneself, the Providence moves, too. All sorts of things occur to help that would never otherwise have occurred. A stream of events issues from the decision, raising unforeseen incidents and meetings and material assistance, which no man could have dreamt would have come his way.

—W.H. Murray

There is no strong performance without a little fanaticism in the performer.

—Ralph Waldo Emerson

Perform without fail what you resolve.

—Benjamin Franklin

Whatsoever thy hand findeth to do, do it
with thy might.

—The Bible, Ecclesiastes

We can do whatever we wish to do pro-
vided our wish is strong enough. But the
tremendous effort needed—one doesn't
always want to make it—does one? …
But what else can be done? What's the
alternative? What do you want most to
do? That's what I have to keep asking
myself, in the face of difficulties.

—Katherine Mansfield

What one has, one ought to use; and
whatever he does, he should do with all
his might.

—Cicero

If you don't wake up with something in
your stomach every day that makes you
think, "I want to make this movie," it'll
never get made.

—Sherry Lansing

Nothing of worthy or weight can be achieved with half a mind, with a faint heart, and with a lame endeavor.

—Isaac Barrow

To have no loyalty is to have no dignity, and in the end, no manhood.

—Peter Taylor Forsyth

He that rides his hobby gently must always give way to him that rides his hobby hard.

—Ralph Waldo Emerson

If you are ashamed to stand by your colors, you had better seek another flag.

—Unknown

Firmness of purpose is one of the most necessary sinews of character, and one of the best instruments of success. Without it, genius wastes its efforts in a maze of inconsistencies.

—Lord Chesterfield

To say yes, you have to sweat and roll up your sleeves and plunge both hands into life up to the elbows. It is easy to say no, even if saying no means death.

—Jean Anouilh

My face is set, my gait is fast, my goal is Heaven, my road is narrow, my way is rough, my companions are few, my guide is reliable, my mission is clear. I cannot be bought, compromised, detoured, lured away, turned back, diluted, or delayed. I will not flinch in the face of sacrifice, hesitate in the presence of adversity, negotiate ... at the table of the enemy, ponder at the pool of popularity, or meander in a maze of mediocrity. I won't give up, shut up, let up, or slow up.

—Robert Moorehead

Great minds have purposes, others have wishes.

—Washington Irving

I don't want people who want to dance, I want people who *have* to dance.

—George Balanchine

Happy are those who dream dreams and are ready to pay the price to make them come true.

—L.J. Cardinal Suenens

I am in earnest; I will not equivocate; I will not excuse; I will not retreat a single inch; and I *will* be heard.

—William Lloyd Garrison

What a man wants to do he generally can do, if he wants to badly enough.

—Louis L'Amour

Never grow a wishbone, daughter, where your backbone ought to be.

—Clementine Paddleford

He turns not back who is bound to a star.

—Leonardo da Vinci

You can't *try* to do things; you simply must *do* them.

—Ray Bradbury

One advantage of marriage, it seems to me, is that when you fall out of love with him, or he falls out of love with you, it keeps you together until you maybe fall in love again.

—Judith Viorst

PART FIVE

CONCENTRATION

THE IMPORTANCE OF CONCENTRATION

To be able to concentrate for a considerable time is essential to difficult achievement.

—Bertrand Russell

It is only when I dally with what I am about, look back and aside, instead of keeping my eyes straight forward, that I feel these cold sinkings of the heart.

—Sir Walter Scott

If I have ever made any valuable discoveries, it has been owing more to patient attention than to any other talent.

—Isaac Newton

If there is anything that can be called genius, it consists chiefly in the ability to give that attention to a subject which keeps it steadily in the mind, till we have surveyed it accurately on all sides.

—Thomas Reid

Nothing interferes with my concentration. You could put on an orgy in my office and I wouldn't look up. Well, maybe once.

—Isaac Asimov

The ability to concentrate and to use your time well is everything.

—Lee Iacocca

The secret of concentration is the secret of self-discovery. You reach inside yourself to discover your personal resources, and what it takes to match them to the challenge.

—Arnold Palmer

If you don't concentrate, you'll end up on your rear.

—Tai Babilonia

A straight path never leads anywhere except to the objective.

—Andre Gide

For him who has no concentration, there is no tranquility.

—Bhagaved Gita

The secret to success in any human endeavor is total concentration.

—Kurt Vonnegut

Don't Try to Do
Too Many Things

Beware of dissipating your powers; strive
constantly to concentrate them.

>—Johann von Goethe

One arrow does not bring down two birds.

>—Turkish proverb

No horse gets anywhere until he is har-
nessed. No steam or gas ever drives anything until it is confined. No Niagara is
ever turned into light and power until it
is tunneled. No life ever grows great until
it is focused, dedicated, disciplined.

>—Harry Emerson Fosdick

A man may be so much of everything
that he is nothing of everything.

>—Samuel Johnson

One cannot both feast and become rich.

>—Ashanti proverb

Concentrate your energies, your thoughts and your capital.... The wise man puts all his eggs in one basket and watches the basket.

—Andrew Carnegie

One man; two loves. No good ever comes of that.

—Euripides

The perplexity of life arises from there being too many interesting things in it for us to be interested properly in any of them.

—G.K. Chesterton

No country can act wisely simultaneously in every part of the globe at every moment of time.

—Henry Kissinger

CONCENTRATE ON ONE THING

The field of consciousness is tiny. It accepts only one problem at a time.
>—Antoine de Saint-Exupery

Successful minds work like a gimlet, to a single point.
>—Christian Bovee

All good is gained by those whose thought and life are kept pointed close to one main thing, not scattered abroad upon a thousand.
>—Stephen McKenna

Give me a man who says this one thing I do, and not these fifty things I dabble in.
>—Dwight L. Moody

A bird can roost but on one branch. A mouse can drink no more than its fill from a river.
>—Chinese proverb

Each man is capable of doing one thing well. If he attempts several, he will fail to achieve distinction in any.

—Plato

To do two things at once is to do neither.
—Publilius Syrus

The first law of success … is concentration: to bend all the energies to one point, and to go directly to that point, looking neither to the right nor the left.
—William Matthews

A single idea, if it is right, saves us the labor of an infinity of experiences.
—Jacques Maritain

Purity of heart is to will one thing.
—Søren Kierkegaard

One thought driven home is better than three left on base.
—James Liter

Eliminate the Non-Essential

A man should remove not only unnecessary acts, but also unnecessary thoughts, for
then superfluous activity will not follow.
>—Marcus Aurelius

Many people who wonder why they
don't amount to more than they do have
good stuff in them, and are energetic,
persevering, and have ample opportunities. It is all a case of trimming the useless branches and throwing the whole
force of power into the development of
something that counts.
>—Walter J. Johnston

A great man is one who seizes the vital
issue in a complex question, what we
might call the jugular vein of the whole
organism, and spends his energies upon
that.
>—Joseph Rickaby

ALWAYS FOCUS ON THE IMMEDIATE TASK

While the work or play is on ... don't constantly feel you ought to be doing the other.

—Franklin P. Adams

When one is learning, one should not think of play; and when one is at play, one should not think of learning.

—Lord Chesterfield

When walking, walk. When eating, eat.

—Zen Maxim

If you want to hit a bird on the wing you must have all your will in focus, you must not be thinking about yourself and, equally, you must not be thinking about your neighbor: you must be living in your eye on that bird. Every achievement is a bird on the wing.

—Oliver Wendell Holmes Jr.

The immature mind hops from one
thing to another; the mature mind seeks
to follow through.

—Harry A. Overstreet

I go at what I am about as if there was
nothing else in the world for the time
being.

—Charles Lingsley

Concentration is everything. On the day
I'm performing, I don't hear anything
anyone says to me.

—Luciano Pavarotti

If you direct your whole thought to work
itself, none of the things which invade
eyes or ears will reach the mind.

—Quintilian

Choice of attention, to pay attention to
this and ignore that, is to the inner life
what choice of action is to the outer.

—W.H. Auden

The real essence of work is concentrated
energy.

—Walter Begehot

I've learned ruthless concentration. I can
write under any circumstances ... street
noises, loud talk, music, you name it.

—Sylvia Porter

The difference in men does not lie in the
size of their hands, nor in the perfection
of their bodies, but in this one sublime
ability of concentration: to throw the
weight with the blow, to live an eternity
in an hour.

—Elbert Hubbard

Do whatever you do intensely.

—Robert Henri

The effectiveness of work increases
according to geometrical progression if
there are no interruptions.

—Andre Maurois

Other people's interruptions of your work are relatively insignificant compared with the countless times you interrupt yourself.

—Brendan Francis

A full mind is an empty baseball bat.
—Branch Rickey

There is time enough for everything in the course of the day if you do but one thing at once; but there is not time enough in the year if you will do two things at a time.

—Lord Chesterfield

You can't ring the bells and, at the same time, walk in the procession.
—Spanish proverb

OTHER SOURCES OF CONCENTRATION

If you direct your whole thought to work
itself, none of the things which invade
eyes or ears will reach the mind.

—Quintilian

Become so wrapped up in something
that you forget to be afraid.

—Lady Bird Johnson

Attention to a subject depends upon our
interest in it.

—Tryon Edwards

I can't concentrate on golf or bowling.
Those bowling pins aren't going to hurt
me. I can concentrate in the ring because
someone is trying to kill me.

—Carmen Basilio

Concentrate on finding your goal, then
concentrate on reaching it.

—Colonel Michael Friedsman

Those who set out to serve both God
and Mammon soon discover that there is
no God.

—Logan Pearsall Smith

When I come into a game in the bottom
of the ninth, bases loaded, no one out
and a one-run lead ... it takes people off
my mind.

—Tug McGraw

When a man knows he is to be hanged
in a fortnight, it concentrates his mind
wonderfully.

—Samuel Johnson

PART SIX

WORK

WORK IS ESSENTIAL TO MOST
PEOPLE'S HAPPINESS

The road to happiness lies in two simple
principles: find what it is that interests
you and that you can do well, and when
you find it, put your whole soul into it—
every bit of energy and ambition and
natural ability you have.
                    —John D. Rockefeller III

After fifty years of living, it occurs to me
that the most significant thing that people do is go to work, whether it is to go
to work on their novel or at the assembly
plant or fixing somebody's teeth.
                        —Thomas McGuane

The happy people are those who are producing something.
                    —William Ralph Inge

Congenial labor is essence of happiness.
                    —Arthur Christopher Benson

The fun of being alive is realizing that you have a talent and you can use it every day, so it grows stronger.... And if you're in an atmosphere where this talent is appreciated instead of just tolerated, why, it's just as good as sex.

—Lou Centlivre

Employment is nature's physician, and is essential to human happiness.

—Galen

There are certain natures to whom work is nothing, the act of work everything.

—Arthur Symons

It is only when I am doing my work that I feel truly alive. It is like having sex.

—Federico Fellini

He who labors diligently need never despair, for all things are accomplished by diligence and labor.

—Menander

Work! Thank God for the swing of it, for the clamoring, hammering ring of it.
—Unknown

Continuity of purpose is one of the most essential ingredients of happiness in the long run, and for most men this comes chiefly through their work.
—Bertrand Russell

When I stop [working], the rest of the day is posthumous. I'm only really alive when I'm working.
—Tennessee Williams

All Work Has Dignity

There's no labor a man can do that's
undignified, if he does it right.

—Bill Cosby

If a man is called to be a streetsweeper,
he should sweep streets even as
Michelangelo painted, or Beethoven
composed music or Shakespeare wrote
poetry. He should sweep streets so well
that all the hosts of heaven and earth will
pause to say, here lived a great
streetsweeper who did his job well.

—Martin Luther King Jr.

Originality and the feeling of one's own
dignity are achieved only through work
and struggle.

—Fyodor Dostoyevsky

There is a kind of victory in good work,
no matter how humble.

—Jack Kemp

The work praises the man.

—Irish proverb

The highest reward for man's toil is not what he gets for it, but what he becomes by it.

—John Ruskin

A professional is someone who can do his best work when he doesn't feel like it.

—Alistair Cooke

Labor disgraces no man; unfortunately, you occasionally find men who disgrace labor.

—Ulysses S. Grant

Honest labor bears a lovely face.

—Thomas Dekker

I have friends in overalls whose friendship I would not swap for the favor of the kings of the world.

—Thomas A. Edison

The world is moved not only by the mighty shoves of the heroes, but also by the aggregate of the tiny pushes of each honest worker.

—Helen Keller

THE IMPORTANCE OF FINDING THE WORK WE WERE MEANT TO DO

Starting out to make money is the greatest mistake in life. Do what you feel you have a flair for doing, and if you are good enough at it, the money will come
—Greer Garson

Never desert your own line of talent. Be what nature intended you for, and you will succeed.
—Sydney Smith

Everybody undertakes what he sees another successful in, whether he has the aptitude for it or not.
—Johann von Goethe

Men whose trade is rat-catching love to catch rats; the bug destroyer seizes on his bug with delight; the suppressor is gratified by finding his vice.
—Sydney Smith

Some people are born to lift heavy weights,
some are born to juggle golden balls.

—Max Beerbohm

Men take only their needs into consideration, never their abilities.

—Napoleon Bonaparte

One should stick to the sort of thing for which one was made; I tried to be an herbalist, whereas I should keep to the butcher's trade.

—Jean de La Fontaine

One principal reason why men are so often useless is that they neglect their own profession or calling, and divide and shift their attention among a multitude of objects and pursuits.

—Nathaniel Emmons

They are happy men whose natures sort with their vocations.

—Francis Bacon

Life is to be lived. If you have to support yourself, you had bloody well better find some way that is going to be interesting. And you don't do that by sitting around wondering about yourself.

—Katharine Hepburn

To find out what one is fitted to do, and to secure an opportunity to do it, is the key to happiness.

—John Dewey

The high prize of life, the crowning fortune of man, is to be born with a bias to some pursuit which finds him in employment and happiness.

—Ralph Waldo Emerson

Work You Love Isn't Work

The test of a vocation is the love of the drudgery it involves.

> —Logan Pearsall Smith

Whenever it is possible, a boy should choose some occupation which he should do even if he did not need the money.

> —William Lyon Phelps

I love Mickey Mouse more than any woman I've ever known.

> —Walt Disney

Only he is successful in his business who makes that pursuit which affords him the highest pleasure sustain him.

> —Henry David Thoreau

When men are rightly occupied, their amusement grows out of their work, as the color-petals out of a fruitful flower.

> —John Ruskin

Give me a man who sings at his work.
                              —Thomas Carlyle

To love what you do and feel that it matters—how could anything be more fun?
                              —Katharine Graham

When love and skill work together,
expect a masterpiece.
                              —John Ruskin

Work consists of whatever a body is
obliged to do, and play consists of whatever a body is not obliged to do.
                              —Mark Twain

Work and play are words used to
describe the same thing under differing
conditions.
                              —Mark Twain

The more I want to get something done,
the less I call it work.
                              —Richard Bach

WORK AND SUCCESS

Nothing worthwhile comes easily. Half effort does not produce half results, it produces no results. Work, continuous work and hard work, is the only way to accomplish results that last.

—Hamilton Holt

If a man wakes up famous, he hasn't been sleeping.

—Wes Izzard

Success is dependent on effort.

—Sophocles

Striving for success without hard work is like trying to harvest where you haven't planted.

—David Bly

Success comes before work only in the dictionary.

—Unknown

Sweat plus sacrifice equals success.
                    —Charles O. Finley

Success usually comes to those who are
too busy to be looking for it.
                    —Henry David Thoreau

In all human affairs there are *efforts,* there
are *results,* and the strength of the effort
is the measure of the result.
                    —James Lane Allen

Work Pays Dividends

Diligence is the mother of good luck,
and God gives all things to industry.
—Benjamin Franklin

To industry, nothing is impossible.
—Latin proverb

Fortune is ever seen accompanying
industry.
—Oliver Goldsmith

Manual labor to my father was not only
good and decent for its own sake, but as
he was given to saying, it straightened
out one's thoughts.
—Mary Ellen Chase

I get satisfaction of three kinds. One is
creating something, one is being paid for
it and one is the feeling that I haven't just
been sitting on my ass all afternoon.
—William F. Buckley

GENERAL QUOTATIONS ABOUT WORK

If you could once make up your mind
never to undertake more work … than
you can carry on calmly, quietly, without
hurry or flurry … and if the instant you
feel yourself growing nervous and … out
of breath, you would stop and take a
breath, you would find this simple com-
mon-sense rule doing for you what no
prayers or tears could ever accomplish.
—Elizabeth Prentiss

Any man who has had the job I've had
and didn't have a sense of humor would-
n't still be here.
—Harry S. Truman

The heights by great men reached and
   kept
Were not attained by sudden flight,
But they, while their companions slept,
Were toiling upward in the night.
—Henry Wadsworth Longfellow

There is no more dreadful punishment
than futile and hopeless labor.

—Albert Camus

Be strong!
We are not here to play, to dream, to
     drift;
We have hard work to do and loads to
     lift;
Shun not the struggle—face it; 'tis God's
     gift.

—Maltbie D. Babcock

It is better to have no emotion when it is
work. Do what needs to be done, and do
it coolly.

—Louis L'Amour

A man's work is from sun to sun, but a
mother's work is never done.

—Unknown

Elbow grease is the best polish.

—English proverb

What a man accomplishes in a day depends upon the way in which he approaches his tasks. When we accept tough jobs as a challenge to our ability and wade into them with joy and enthusiasm, miracles can happen. When we do our work with a dynamic, conquering spirit, we get things done.

—Arland Gilbert

The one important thing I have learned over the years is the difference between taking one's work seriously, and taking one's self seriously. The first is imperative, and the second is disastrous.

—Margot Fonteyn

Industry is a better horse to ride than genius. —Walter Lippman

Opportunity is missed by most people because it is dressed in overalls, and looks like work.

—Thomas A. Edison

Work is the best method devised for killing time.

— William Feather

Laziness is a secret ingredient that goes into failure. But it's only kept a secret from the person who fails.

— Robert Half

Never despair, but if you do, work on in despair.

— Edmund Burke

PART SEVEN

PERFECTION

NOTHING IS PERFECT

Perfection does not exist. To understand this is the triumph of human intelligence; to expect to possess it is the most dangerous kind of madness.

—Alfred de Musset

The essence of man is imperfection.

—Norman Cousins

The essence of being human is that one does not seek perfection.

—George Orwell

There is no perfection in humanity.

—Samuel Montagne

Perfection never exists in reality, but only in our dreams.

—Dr. Rudolf Dreikurs

He is lifeless that is faultless.

—English proverb

His only fault is that he has no fault.

—Pliny, the Younger

If you're looking for perfection, look in the mirror. If you find it there, expect it elsewhere.

—Malcolm Forbes

A perfect poem is impossible. Once it has been written, the world would end.

—Robert Graves

It is the function of perfection to make one know one's imperfection.

—Saint Augustine

A man would do nothing if he waited until he could do it so well that no one could find fault.

—John Henry Cardinal Newman

The man with insight enough to admit his limitations comes nearest to perfection.

—Johann von Goethe

Perfection is out of the question.
　　　　　　　—Anne Archer

Angels can do no better.
　　　　　　　—K. Panuthos

Nothing you write, if you hope to be any
good, will ever come out as you first
hoped.
　　　　　　　—Lillian Hellman

All of us failed to match our dreams of
perfection.
　　　　　　　—William Faulkner

What, after all, is a halo? It's only one
more thing to keep clean.
　　　　　　　—Christopher Fry

We Don't Need to Be Perfect

To talk about the need for perfection in
man is to talk about the need for another
species.

—Norman Cousins

Striving for perfection is the greatest
stopper there is. You'll be afraid you can't
achieve it.… It's your excuse to yourself
for not doing anything. Instead, strive for
excellence, doing your best.

—Sir Laurence Olivier

You know what they call the guy who
finishes last in medical school? They call
him Doctor!

—Abe Lemons

The "C" students run the world.

—Harry S. Truman

A good garden may have some weeds.

—Thomas Fuller

Perfection is no more a requisite to art
than to heroes.

—Ned Rorem

At times failure is very necessary for the
artist. It reminds him that failure is not
the ultimate disaster. And this reminder
liberates him from the mean fussing of
perfectionism.

—John Berger

PEOPLE DON'T EXPECT OR WANT PERFECTION

Living with a saint is more grueling than being one.

> —Robert Neville

He is all fault who hath no fault at all. For who loves me must have a touch of earth.

> —Alfred, Lord Tennyson

You're only human, you're supposed to make mistakes.

> —Billy Joel

I don't like a man to be too efficient. He's likely to be not human enough.

> —Felix Frankfurter

I like a man with faults, especially when he knows it. To err is human—I'm uncomfortable around gods.

> —Hugh Prather

Sainthood is acceptable only in saints.
—Pamela Hansford Johnson

If the best man's faults were written on his forehead, it would make him pull his hat over his eyes.

—Gaelic proverb

Friendships aren't perfect, and yet they are very precious. For me, not expecting perfection all in one place was a great release.

—Letty Cottin Pogrebin

IT ISN'T HEALTHY TO SEEK PERFECTION

The man who makes no mistakes lacks boldness and the spirit of adventure. He never tries anything new. He is a brake on the wheels of progress.

—M.W. Larmour

A concern with the perfectibility of mankind is always a symptom of thwarted or perverted development.

—Hugh Kingsmill

When everything has to be right, something isn't.

—Stanislaw Lec

The maxim "Nothing avails but perfection" may be spelled "Paralysis."

—Sir Winston Churchill

Perfectionism is slow death.

—Hugh Prather

Perfectionism is a dangerous state of mind in an imperfect world.

—Robert Hillyer

Perfect order is the forerunner of perfect horror.

—Carlos Fuentes

The more a human being feels himself a self, tries to intensify this self and reach a never-attainable perfection, the more drastically he steps out of the center of being.

—Eugene Herrigel

WE JUST NEED TO DO
THE BEST WE CAN

Use what talents you have; the woods
would have little music if no birds sang
their song except those who sang best.
—Reverend Oliver G. Wilson

Even a clock that is not going is right
twice a day.

—Polish proverb

Have patience with all things, but chiefly
have patience with yourself. Do not lose
courage in considering your own imper-
fections, but instantly set about remedy-
ing them—every day begin the task anew.
—Saint Francis de Sales

I'll take any way to get into the Hall of
Fame. If they want a batboy, I'll go in as
a batboy.

—Phil Rizzuto

We're the best team in baseball. But not by much.

—Sparky Anderson,
after winning the World Series

I only have to stop the puck, not beat it to death.

—Don Beaupre, hockey goalie

General Quotations about Perfection

One must not hold one's self so divine as to be unwilling occasionally to make improvements in one's creations.

—Ludwig van Beethoven

The artist who aims at perfection in everything achieves it in nothing.

—Eugene Delacroix

You just have to learn not to care about the dust mites under the beds.

—Margaret Mead

PART EIGHT

JUST DO IT

ACTION

Having the world's best idea will do you no good unless you act on it. People who want milk shouldn't sit on a stool in the middle of a field in hopes that a cow will back up to them.

—Curtis Grant

Ideas are powerful things, requiring not a studious contemplation but an action, even if it is only an inner action.

—Midge Dector

There is no genius in life like the genius of energy and activity.

—Donald G. Mitchell

The only measure of what you believe is what you do. If you want to know what people believe, don't read what they write, don't ask them what they believe, just observe what they do.

—Ashley Montagu

The only way to get positive feelings about yourself is to take positive actions. Man does not live as he thinks, he thinks as he lives.
—Reverend Vaughan Quinn, O.M.I.

Life happens at the level of events, not words.
—Alfred Adler

Let us work as if success depended upon ourselves alone, but with heartfelt conviction that we are doing nothing, and God everything.
—Saint Ignatius Loyola

Our nature consists in motion; complete rest is death.
—Blaise Pascal

Who can separate his faith from his actions, or his belief from his occupations?
—Kahlil Gibran

The prayer of the chicken hawk does not get him the chicken.
—Swahili proverb

The superior man is modest in his speech, but excels in his actions.

—Confucius

Inspirations never go in for long engagements; they demand immediate marriage to action.

—Brendan Francis

The life of the spirit is centrally and essentially a life of action. Spiritu-ality is something done, not merely something believed, or known or experienced.

—Mary McDermott Shideler

An ounce of action is worth a ton of theory.

—Friedrich Engels

Action is the only reality, not only reality but morality, as well.

—Abbie Hoffman

Right action is the key to good living.

—*Twelve Steps and Twelve Traditions*

Even if you're on the right track, you'll get run over if you just sit there.

—Will Rogers

If faith without works is dead, willingness without action is fantasy.

—Unknown

The door of opportunity won't open unless you do some pushing.

—Unknown

It is a great piece of skill to know how to guide your luck, even while waiting for it.

—Baltasar Gracian

The man who has done nothing but wait for his ship to come in has already missed the boat.

—Unknown

God doesn't make orange juice, God makes oranges.

—Jesse Jackson

WE'RE RESPONSIBLE FOR THE
EFFORT—NOT THE OUTCOME

Learn to do thy part and leave the rest to
Heaven.

—John Henry Cardinal Newman

Trust in God and *do* something.

—Mary Lyon

God helps them that helps themselves.

—Benjamin Franklin

He will hew the line of right, let the
chips fall where they may.

—Roscoe Conklin

Let me win, but if I cannot win, let me
be brave in the attempt.

—Motto of the Special Olympics

Doing what's right is no guarantee
against misfortune.

—William McFee

We cannot merely pray to You, O God,
     to end war;
For we know that You have made the
     world in a way
That man must find his own path to peace
Within himself, and with his neighbor.
                                    —Jack Riemer

Oh Lord, thou givest us everything, at
the price of an effort.
                                    —Leonardo da Vinci

On God for all events depend;
You cannot want when God's your friend.
Weigh well your part and do your best;
Leave to your Maker all the rest.
                                    —Nathaniel Cotton

Life has ... taught me not to expect success to be the inevitable result of my
endeavors. She taught me to seek suste-
nance from the endeavor itself, but to
leave the result to God.
                                    —Alan Paton

You, yourself, must make the effort. The buddhas are only teachers.

—Buddhist proverb

There is a time for all things; a time to preach and a time to pray, but those times have passed away; there is a time to fight, *and that time has come!*

—General Peter Muhlenberg

It is not yours to finish the task, but neither are you free to take no part in it.

—Unknown

'Tis man's to fight, but Heaven's to give success.

—Homer

That man is blest who does his best and leaves the rest; do not worry.

—Charles F. Deems

God alone can finish.

—John Ruskin

If people are suffering, then they must
look within themselves.... Happiness is
not something ready-made [Buddha] can
give you. It comes from your own actions.
—The Dalai Lama

I am not bound to win, but
I am bound to be true.
I am not bound to succeed, but
I am bound to live up to what light I have.
—Abraham Lincoln

God hasn't called me to be successful.
He's called me to be faithful.
—Mother Teresa

Happy people plan actions, they don't
plan results.
—Dennis Wholey

No way exists in the present to accurately
determine the future effect of the least of
our actions.
—Gerald Jampolsky

In vain our labours are, whatsoe'er they be, unless God gives the Benediction.
—Robert Herrick

In all human affairs there are *efforts,* and there are results, and the strength of the effort is the measure of the result.
—James Lane Allen

An act of love that fails is just as much a part of the divine life as an act of love that succeeds, for love is measured by its own fullness, not by its reception.
—Harold Loukes

On earth we have nothing to do with success or results, but only with being true to God, and for God. Defeat in doing right is nevertheless victory
—F.W. Robertson

Try first thyself, and after call in God, For to the worker God himself lends aid.
—Euripides

The man who has done his level best,
and who is conscious that he has done
his best, is a success, even though the
world may write him down a failure.
—B.C. Forbes

To create is to boggle the mind and alter
the mood. Once the urge has surged, it
maintains its own momentum. We may go
along for the ride, but when we attempt to
steer the course, the momentum dies.
—Sue Atchley Ebaugh

If thou workest at that which is before thee
... expecting nothing, fearing nothing, but
satisfied with thy present activity according
to Nature, and with heroic truth in every
word and sound which thou utterest, thou
wilt live happy. And there is no man
who is able to prevent this.
—Marcus Aurelius

We Can't—and Don't Need to—Control Things

You have striven so hard, and so long, to *compel* life. Can't you now slowly change, and let life slowly drift into you ... let the invisible life steal into you and slowly possess you.

—D.H. Lawrence

Relinquishing control is the ultimate challenge of the Spiritual Warrior.

—*The Book of Runes*

I began to have an idea of my life, not as the slow shaping of achievement to fit my preconceived purposes, but as the gradual discovery and growth of a purpose which I did not know

—Joanna Field

The bird of paradise alights only upon the hand that does not grasp.

—John Berry

A guru might say that spiritual deepening involves a journey toward the unselfconscious living of life as it unfolds, rather than toward a willful determination to make it happen.

—John Fortunato

As the soft yield of water cleaves obstinate stone,
So to yield with life solves the insolvable:
To yield, I have learned, is to come back again

—Lao-tzu

Living upon a basis of unsatisfied demands, we were in a state of continual disturbance and frustration. Therefore, no peace was to be had unless we could find a means of reducing these demands.
—*Twelve Steps and Twelve Traditions*

You have freedom when you're easy in your harness.

—Robert Frost

Somehow, when we no longer feel in control, we become available to deeper aliveness.

—Richard Moss

Life is made up of desires that seem big and vital one minute, and little and absurd the next. I guess we get what's best for us in the end.

—Alice Caldwell Rice

As your faith is strengthened, you will find that there is no longer the need to have a sense of control, that things will flow as they will, and that you will flow with them, to your great delight and benefit.

—Emmanuel

It had been my repeated experience that when you said to life calmly and firmly (but very firmly!), "I trust you; do what you must," life had an uncanny way of responding to your need.

—Olga Ilyin

Eventually I lost interest in trying to control my life, to make things happen in a way that I thought I wanted them to be. I began to practice surrendering to the universe and finding out what "it" wanted me to do.

—Shakti Gawain

Men never cling to their dreams with such tenacity as at the moment when they are losing faith in them, and know it, but do not dare yet to confess it to themselves.

—W.G. Sumner

So often we try to alter circumstances to suit ourselves, instead of letting them alter us.

—Mother Maribel

Willfulness must give way to willingness and surrender. Mastery must yield to mystery.

—Gerald G. May

For peace of mind, resign as general manager of the universe.

—Unknown

The worst thing you can do is to try to cling to something that's gone, or to recreate it.

—Johnette Napolitano

I claim not to have controlled events, but confess plainly that events have controlled me.

—Abraham Lincoln

Letting people be okay without us is how we get to be okay without them.

—Merrit Malloy

WE ARE INSTRUMENTS OF GOD

We are the wire, God is the current. Our only power is to let the current pass through us.

—Carlo Carretto

I am like a little pencil in God's hand. He does the writing. The pencil has nothing to do with it.

—Mother Teresa

There are two kinds of people: those who say to God, "Thy will be done," and those to whom God says, "All right, then, have it your way."

—C.S. Lewis

Here am I; send me.

—*The Bible, Isaiah*

'Tis God gives skill, but not without men's hands: he could not make Antonio Stradivarius violins without Antonio.

—George Eliot

WE MUST TRUST OUR
HIGHER POWER

Life is God's novel. Let him write it.
>   —Isaac Bashevis Singer

To character and success, two things, con-
tradictory as they may seem, must go
together—humble dependence and
manly independence: humble dependence
on God, and manly reliance on self.
>   —William Wordsworth

Whate'er we leave to God, God does and
blesses us.
>   —Henry David Thoreau

God will help you if you try, and you can
if you think you can.
>   —Anna Delaney Peale

Doing what is right isn't the problem; it's
knowing what is right.
>   —Lyndon B. Johnson

Let each look to himself and see what
God wants of him and attend to this,
leaving all else alone.

—Henry Suso

God tests His real friends more severely
than the lukewarm ones.

—Katheryn Hulme

In vain our labours are, whatsoe'er they
be, unless God gives the Benediction.

—Robert Herrick

Much that I sought, I could not find;
much that I found, I could not bind;
much that I bound, I could not free;
much that I freed, returned to me.

—Lee Wilson Dodd

If you can't help it, don't think about it.

—Carmel Myers

God alone can finish.

—John Ruskin

Wanna fly, you got to give up the shit
that weighs you down.

—Toni Morrison

Do not inflict your will.
Just give love.
The soul will take that love and put it
    where it can best be used.

—Emmanuel

Be God or let God.

—Unknown

With us is the Lord our God, to help us
and to fight our battles.

—The Bible, II Chronicles

It is better to trust in the Lord than to
put confidence in man.

—The Bible, Psalms

Cast your burden on the Lord, and he
shall sustain you.

—The Bible, Psalms

But I trusted in thee, O Lord; I said, Thou
art my God. My times are in thy hand.
—The Bible, Psalms

God's will is not an itinerary, but an
attitude.
—Andrew Dhuse

Trust in the Lord with all your heart, and
lean not on your own understanding; in
all your ways acknowledge Him, and He
shall direct your paths.
—The Bible, Proverbs

Casting all your care upon Him, for He
cares for you.
—The Bible, I Peter

My life is … a mystery which I do not
attempt to really understand, as though I
were led by the hand in a night where I see
nothing, but can fully depend on the love
and protection of Him who guides me.
—Thomas Merton

Be like the bird that, passing on her
flight awhile on boughs too slight, feels
them give way beneath her, and yet sings,
knowing that she hath wings.

—Victor Hugo

I come to the office each morning and
stay for long hours doing what has to be
done to the best of my ability. And when
you've done the best you can, you can't
do any better. So when I go to sleep I
turn everything over to the Lord and forget it.

—Harry S. Truman

Even now I am full of hope, but the end
lies in God. —Pindar

PART NINE

ONE STEP AT A TIME

BIG THINGS ARE ACCOMPLISHED
ONE STEP AT A TIME

When you have a great and difficult task,
something perhaps almost impossible, if
you only work a little at a time, every day
a little, suddenly the work will finish itself.

—Isak Dinesen

Look at a stone cutter hammering away
at his rock, perhaps a hundred times
without as much as a crack showing in it.
Yet at the hundred-and-first blow it will
split in two, and I know it was not the
last blow that did it, but all that had
gone before.

—Jacob A. Riis

All that I have accomplished … has been
by that plodding, patient, persevering
process of accretion which builds the ant
heap particle by particle, thought by
thought, fact by fact.

—Elihu Burritt

Not to go back is somewhat to advance.
And men must walk, at least, before they
dance.

—Alexander Pope

Great things are not done by impulse, but
by a series of small things brought together.
—Vincent van Gogh

Nothing is particularly hard if you divide
it into small jobs.

—Henry Ford

Many things which cannot be overcome
when they are together, yield themselves
up when taken little by little. —Plutarch
True worth is doing each day some little
good, not dreaming of great things to do
by and by.

—Unknown

Well-being is attained little by little, and
is no little thing itself.

—Zeno of Citium

Bigness comes from doing many small things well.... Individually, they are not very dramatic transactions. Together, though, they add up.

—Edward S. Finkelstein

Little drops of water, little grains of sand,
Make the mighty ocean, and the pleasant
  land:
So the little minutes, humble though
  they be,
Make the mighty ages of eternity.
Little deeds of kindness, little words of
  love,
Help to make earth happy, like Heaven
  up above.

—Julia Carney

Little by little does the trick.

—Aesop

One thing at a time, all things in succession. That which grows slowly endures.

—J.G. Hubbard

It is by attempting to reach the top at a
single leap that so much misery is caused
in the world.

—William Cobbett

He who would learn to fly one day must
first learn to stand and walk and run and
climb and dance; one cannot fly into flying.

—Friedrich Nietzsche

I think and think for months, for years.
Ninety-nine times the conclusion is false.
The hundredth time I am right.

—Albert Einstein

It is a mistake to look too far ahead.
Only one link in the chain of destiny can
be handled at a time.

—Sir Winston Churchill

A successful individual typically sets his
next goal somewhat, but not too much,
above his last achievement.

—Kurt Lewin

Yesterday I dared to struggle. Today I dare to win.

—Bernadette Devlin

If you only keep adding little by little, it will soon become a big heap.

—Hesiod

Many strokes overthrow the tallest oaks.

—John Luly

Much rain wears the marble.

—William Shakespeare

SMALL STEPS ARE BIG DEALS

One sits down first; one thinks afterwards.
—Jean Cocteau

Many strokes, though with a little axe, hew
down and fell the hardest-timber'd oak.
—William Shakespeare

Progress is the sum of small victories won
by individual human beings.
—Bruce Catton

What saves a man is to take a step. Then
another step.
—Antoine de Saint-Exupery

The waters wear the stones.
—The Bible, Job

You don't just luck into things.... You
build step by step, whether it's friendships or opportunities.

—Barbara Bush

One step and then another, and the
    longest walk is ended.
One stitch and then another, and the
    longest rent is mended.
One brick upon another, and the tallest
    wall is made.
One flake and then another, and the
    deepest snow is laid.

              —Unknown

The way a Chihuahua goes about eating a
dead elephant is to take a bite and be very
present with that bite. In spiritual growth,
the definitive act is to take one step and
let tomorrow's step take care of itself!

              —William H. Houff

Inches Add Up

Victory is won not in miles, but in inches. Win a little now, hold your ground, and later win a little more.

—Louis L'Amour

Inches make a champion.

—Vince Lombardi

If we take care of the inches, we will not have to worry about the miles.

—Hartley Coleridge

Yard by yard, it's very hard. But inch by inch, it's a cinch.

—Unknown

When Ty Cobb got on first base he had an apparently nervous habit of kicking the bag.... Cobb could move it a full two inches closer to second base. He figured that this improved his chances for a steal, or for reaching second base safely on a hit.

—Norman Vincent Peale

LITTLE THINGS ARE BIG THINGS

Most people would succeed in small
things if they were not troubled with
great ambitions.
>—Henry Wadsworth Longfellow

Life is made up of little things. It is very
rarely that an occasion is offered for
doing a great deal at once. True greatness
consists in being great in little things.
>—Charles Simmons

Life is a great bundle of little things.
>—Oliver Wendell Holmes

I recommend you to take care of the
minutes, for the hours will take care of
themselves.
>—Lord Chesterfield

Practice yourself in little things, and
thence proceed to greater.
>—Epictetus

Nothing can be done except little by little.
—Charles Baudelaire

Those people work more wisely who seek
to achieve good in their own small corner
of the world … than those who are forever thinking that life is in vain, unless
one can … do big things.
—Herbert Butterfield

You've got to think about "big things"
while you're doing small things, so that all
the small things go in the right direction.
—Alvin Toffler

Little strokes fell great oaks.
—Benjamin Franklin

Take your needle, my child, and work at
your pattern; it will come out a rose by
and by. Life is like that; one stitch at a
time taken patiently, and the pattern will
come out all right, like embroidery.
—Oliver Wendell Holmes

Most of us miss out on life's big prizes. The Pulitzer. The Nobel. Oscars. Tonys. Emmys. But we're all eligible for life's small pleasures. A pat on the back. A kiss behind the ear. A four-pound bass. A full moon. An empty parking space. A crackling fire. A great meal. A glorious sunset. Hot Soup. Cold beer. Don't fret about copping life's grand awards. Enjoy its tiny delights. There are plenty for all of us.

—United Technologies Corporation advertisement

Why not learn to enjoy the little things—there are so many of them.

—Unknown

The mere sense of living is joy enough.

—Emily Dickinson

How far that little candle throws his beams! So shines a good deed in a naughty world.

—William Shakespeare

Enjoy the little things, for one day you may look back and realize they were the big things.

—Robert Brault

Trifles make up the happiness or the misery of mortal life.

—Alexander Smith

Even a small star shines in the darkness.

—Finnish proverb

It is better to light a candle than to curse the darkness.

—Chinese proverb

The big things that come our way are ... the fruit of seeds planted in the daily routine of our work.

—William Feather

The little things are infinitely the most important.

—A. Conan Doyle

If you don't enjoy getting up and working and finishing your work and sitting
down to a meal with family or friends,
then the chances are you're not going to
be happy. If someone bases his happiness
or unhappiness on major events like a
great new job, huge amounts of money, a
flawlessly happy marriage or a trip to
Paris, that person isn't going to be happy
much of the time. If, on the other hand,
happiness depends on a good breakfast,
flowers in the yard, a drink or a nap,
then we are more likely to live with quite
a bit of happiness.

—Andy Rooney

It is in trifles, and when he is off his guard,
that a man best shows his character.

—Arthur Schopenhauer

Life is denied by lack of attention,
whether it be to cleaning windows or
trying to write a masterpiece.

—Nadia Boulanger

It was only a sunny smile,
But it scattered the night
And little it cost in the giving;
Like morning light,
And made the day worth living.

—Unknown

Put your heart, mind, intellect, and soul
even to your smallest acts. This is the
secret of success.

—Swami Sivananda

The smallest effort is not lost,
Each wavelet on the ocean tost
Aids in the ebb-tide or the flow;
Each rain-drop makes some floweret blow;
Each struggle lessens human woe.

—Charles Mackay

Human felicity is produced not so much
by great pieces of good fortune that
seldom happen as by little advantages
that occur every day.

—Benjamin Franklin

Sometimes the littlest things in life are the hardest to take. You can sit on a mountain more comfortably than on a tack.

—Unknown

In life's small things be resolute and great
To keep thy muscle trained;
Know'st thou when Fate
Thy measure takes, or when she'll say to
    thee,
"I find thee worthy; do this deed for me?"

—James Russell Lowell

He that is faithful in that which is least is faithful also in much; and he that is unjust in the least is unjust also in much.

—The Bible, Luke

We think in generalities, but we live in detail.

—Alfred North Whitehead

JUST DOING WHATEVER WE CAN IS ENOUGH

I cannot do everything, but still I can do something; and because I cannot do everything, I will not refuse to do something that I can do.

—Edward Everett Hale

We cannot do everything at once, but we can do something at once.

—Calvin Coolidge

We must not ... ignore the small daily differences we can make which, over time, add up to big differences that we often cannot foresee.

—Marian Write Edelman

God requires a faithful fulfillment of the merest trifle given us to do, rather than the most ardent aspiration to things to which we are not called.

—Saint Francis de Sales

Nobody makes a greater mistake than he who did nothing because he could only do a little.

—Edmund Burke

MODEST BEGINNINGS CAN LEAD TO GREAT RESULTS

Large streams from little mountains flow,
tall oaks from little acorns grow.
—David Everett

The man who removes a mountain
begins by carrying away small stones.
—Chinese proverb

Start by doing what's necessary, then
what's possible, and suddenly you are
doing the impossible.
—Saint Francis of Assisi

A journey of a thousand miles must
begin with a single step.
—Chinese proverb

No matter how big and tough a problem
may be, get rid of confusion by taking one
little step toward solution. Do *something*.
—George F. Nordenholt

The distance doesn't matter; only the first step is difficult.

  —Madame Marquise du Deffand

A terrace nine stories high begins with a pile of earth.

    —Lao-tzu

Though thy beginning was small, yet thy latter end should greatly increase.

    —The Bible, Job

Almost everything comes from almost nothing.

    —Henri Frederic Amiel

The greatest masterpieces were once only pigments on a palette.

    —Henry S. Haskins

Most of the critical things in life, which become the starting points of human destiny, are little things.

    —R. Smith

From a little spark may burst a mighty flame.

—Dante Alighieri

If you wish to reach the highest, begin at the lowest.

—Publilius Syrus

Great issues develop from small beginnings.
—Norman Vincent Peale

Events of great consequence often spring from trifling circumstances.

—Livy

Sow an act, reap a habit; sow a habit, reap a character; sow a character, reap a destiny.
—G.D. Boardman

The way to succeed is never quit. That's it. But really be humble about it.... You start out lowly and humble and you carefully try to learn an accretion of little things that help you get there.

—Alex Haley

GENERAL QUOTATIONS ABOUT TAKING ONE STEP AT A TIME

There is time enough for everything in the course of the day if you do but one thing once; but there is not time enough in the year if you will do two things at a time.
—Lord Chesterfield

Think not because no man sees, such things will remain unseen.
—Henry Wadsworth Longfellow

Let us then be up and doing,
With a heart for any fate,
Still achieving, still pursuing,
Learn to labor and to wait.
—Henry Wadsworth Longfellow

Every worthwhile accomplishment, big or little, has its stages of drudgery and triumph; a beginning, a struggle, and a victory.
—Unknown

A little neglect may breed great mischief ... For want of a nail, the shoe was lost; for want of a shoe, the horse was lost; for want of a horse, the battle was lost; for want of the battle, the war was lost.
—Benjamin Franklin

The world is moved not only by the mighty shoves of the heroes, but also by the aggregate of the tiny pushes of each honest worker.
—Helen Keller

Inspiration does not come like a blot, nor is it kinetic energy striving, but it comes to us slowly and quietly all the time.
—Brenda Euland

I long to accomplish a great and noble task, but it is my chief duty to accomplish small tasks as if they were great and noble.
—Helen Keller

In great matters men show themselves as
they wish to be seen; in small matters, as
they are.

—Gamaliel Bradford

If, after all, men cannot always make his-
tory have a meaning, they can always act
so that their own lives have one.

—Albert Camus